The
Boer
War

Denis Judd

The Boer War

General Editor:
Ludovic Kennedy

Hart-Davis, MacGibbon
London

Granada Publishing Limited
First published in Great Britain 1977 by Hart-Davis, MacGibbon Ltd
Frogmore, St Albans, Hertfordshire AL2 2NF and
3 Upper James Street, London WIR 4BP

ISBN 0 246 10868 1

Printed in Great Britain by
William Clowes & Sons, Limited
London, Beccles and Colchester

Contents

To Kate, Luke and Ben,
who know all about fighting.

Acknowledgements

Grateful acknowledgement is made for permission to reproduce from the following:
The Great Boer War by Sir Arthur Conan Doyle. Reproduced by permission of Baskervilles Investments Limited.
The Boer War Diary of Sol T. Plaatje edited by John Comaroff. Reproduced by permission of MacMillan South Africa (Publishers).
My Early Life by W. S. Churchill. Reproduced by permission of The Hamlyn Publishing Group Limited.
The photographs and illustrations in this book are reproduced by kind permission of the following. Those on pages 10, 24, 32, 33, 38, 53, 62, 64, 68–9, 73, 76, 84, 85, 88, 90, 103, 104, 106, 108, 128–9, 131, 134, 150, 152, 156, 158, 164, 166, 170 and 181, National Army Museum; pages 2–3, 15, 16, 30–31, 52, 78, 95, 98, 101, 112, 114, 117, 174–5, 177, 179 and 184, Radio Times Hulton Picture Library; pages 35, 44, 46–7, 50, 82, 86, 125, 143, 147, 148 and 160, Imperial War Museum; pages 12–13, 17 and 18, Africana Museum, Johannesburg; pages 21, 22 and 162, National Portrait Gallery, London; pages 26, 56 and 67, Mary Evans Picture Library; pages 36 and 168, The Transvaal Archives; pages 132 and 138, The Mansell Collection; and on page 92, Ikon. Celia Dearing researched the pictures. The maps were drawn by Bucken Limited.

Introduction

The Boer War was Britain's last great imperial war. Contemporary reaction to Joseph Chamberlain's campaign to annex one final piece of Africa for the Empire was accompanied by jingoistic elation, a recognition of the crippling weaknesses of Britain's military machine, and the stirrings of a liberal conscience: perhaps, after all, it would have been better not to have said good-bye to Dolly Gray. As Rudyard Kipling, poet par excellence of the Boer War, wrote in 'The Lesson, 1899–1902':

> Let us admit it fairly as a business people should
> We have had no end of a lesson: it will do us no end of good.

And yet the hostility the war provoked in anti-war campaigners such as Lloyd George, Campbell-Bannerman and Emily Hobhouse, was not simply directed against the disastrous military tactics of Sir Redvers Buller, VC, which, until the relief of Ladysmith, cost thousands of lives and seriously undermined Britain's international standing. It also sprang from a deep sympathy for the stoic Afrikaner farmers who showed astonishing courage and resourcefulness in withstanding the powerful British forces that poured into South Africa in the autumn of 1899. Even after the relief of Kimberley and Mafeking and the fall of Pretoria and Bloemfontein, when the shaken, disillusioned ex-president Kruger saw the Transvaal republic and the Orange Free State smashed to pieces by the British army, an extraordinary guerilla war continued for eighteen months. In it the imaginative exploits of the elusive Christiaan de Wet earned him a hero's welcome when, in August 1902, he came to London to negotiate.

Dr Judd's scholarly and skilful account neither vindicates Chamberlain's imperial policy, nor plays down the magnitude and complications of Britain's subsequent victory. What does emerge is a new disquiet felt at the time about the very nature of warmongering. This is what a war correspondent wrote at the relief of Kimberley:

One found man after man thin, listless and (in spite of the joy of salvation) dispirited, talking with a tired voice and hopeless air, and with a queer, shifty, nervous scared look in the eye … The thing was scarcely human, scarcely of this world. These men were not like oneself.

Fifteen years later, such descriptions were to become commonplace in the carnage of the Western Front.

Chapter 1

An Irrepressible Conflict?
The Origins of the War

The Boer War of 1899–1902 symbolized Britain's towering imperial status and at the same time exposed potentially crippling weaknesses in her military machine. It marked both the apotheosis of her late-nineteenth century Imperial expansion, and also its collapse. The war, like all wars, promoted legends and convenient national myths, and paid scant respect to truth. The British public were told by the government that the war was being fought to protect the Uitlanders of the Transvaal, who were mostly British citizens, from Afrikaner tyranny. The Afrikaners of the Transvaal and the Orange Free State believed that Whitehall, working hand in glove with Cecil Rhodes, had hatched a diabolical plot to strip them of their independence and subordinate them to British Imperial control.

The origins of the war, however, were more complicated than that. Following the Great Trek of the late 1830s, Afrikaner settlers established two republics to the north of Cape Colony: the Orange Free State and the Transvaal. The trekkers had quit the Cape to shake off British rule, which they equated with undue interference with their well established way of life. In particular, the dissident Afrikaners believed that the British administration (which had only recently been established after the Cape's annexation during the Napoleonic Wars) was insensitive to their needs and prone to disregard their prejudices. Seeing themselves as a white Calvinist élite in a black sub-continent, many of the Afrikaners became convinced that their new masters were bent on destroying the social and economic structure of the Cape Colony.

So, fearing racial equality, hungry for more land, and fed on rumours of enforced Catholicism and intermarriage with the Hottentots and Kaffirs, substantial numbers of Cape Dutch (or Afrikaners) migrated across the Orange and Vaal Rivers. The British government eventually decided to recognize the new republics in the early 1850s, while hoping to restrain frontier clashes between the Afrikaners and their Bantu neighbours. To some statesmen, both in Britain and southern Africa, it seemed probable that the white-dominated provinces would one day federate, the Afrikaner republics linking up with the British colonies of the Cape and Natal. Such a federation, however, was to prove elusive.

From 1869 the situation in southern Africa became more complex. The discovery of diamonds in that year at Kimberley, in Bechuanaland, not only gave promise of future mineral findings but also made a millionaire of a sickly young Englishman named Cecil John Rhodes. Eight years later the Zulu menace on the

Opposite Cecil John Rhodes, self-made millionaire, dreamer of dreams of Imperial expansion, and apostle of an Anglo-Saxon global supremacy. He died in 1902.

Perils of the Great Trek, 1836–8, which established the Boer republics beyond the borders of Cape Colony.

borders of the Transvaal gave the British government the pretext for annexing that territory in 1877. The annexation of the Transvaal, however, was a bitter failure, for at the end of 1880 the Transvaalers rose in rebellion, and in January and February 1881 inflicted a series of humiliating defeats upon outnumbered British forces, culminating in the catastrophe of Majuba Hill.

In the aftermath of Majuba, the Gladstone government restored the Transvaal's independence, though also claiming a shadowy suzerainty over the territory. Federation was apparently further away than ever, despite the fact that the Orange Free State had close reciprocal commercial and customs links with the British colonies in South Africa. The most constructive view of Anglo-Afrikaner relations in the early 1880s, therefore, rested on the assumption that commercial self-interest and the need for British military protection against the Bantu would gradually draw the Afrikaner republics into the Imperial sphere of influence. The Transvaal War of 1880–81 had admittedly aroused deep-seated suspicions and antagonisms – but at least the Afrikaners had won the war and regained their independence.

The discovery in 1886 of huge gold deposits in the Transvaal, however, destroyed the chances of a leisurely absorption of the two republics into the Imperial system. The gold strike on the Witwatersrand transformed the sleepy dorp of Johannesburg, within a decade, into a modern, bustling city of fifty thousand European inhabitants. A great gold-mining industry sprang up on the Rand, in almost absurd contrast to the slow, pastoral economy of the rest of the Transvaal.

But the expanding industrial complex based on Johannesburg brought untold riches, and unprecedented problems, to the Transvaal. The gold boom boosted the Transvaal's revenue from £196,000 in 1886 to more than £4 million in 1896. Yet the gold-mining industry had been financed chiefly by British capital, and British technological skills had been needed to dig the precious ore out of the ground. British citizens had thus flooded into Johannesburg and the mining areas, and it was soon reckoned that these foreign immigrants actually outnumbered the Transvaalers. This immigration caused the 'Uitlander problem'. Paul Kruger, the resolute, pious and shrewd president of the Transvaal (formally known as the South African Republic) was determined to keep political power out of the hands of the 'Uitlanders', or 'foreigners'. He thus resolutely refused to accord them full civil rights, including the franchise. Though some Uitlanders were indeed enfranchised, and a few sat in the Volksraad (the Transvaal's

Opposite The 'big hole' at Kimberley, where the discovery of diamonds made Cecil Rhodes a millionaire and a power throughout Africa and the British Empire.

14

Gold-boom city.
Commissioner Street,
Johannesburg, looking
eastwards.

parliament) the vast majority remained unable to vote.

It is easy to understand Kruger's tough stand on the Uitlander question. Given full enfranchisement the Uitlanders might well have voted in an English-speaking government, and achieved the bloodless coup of a revolution through the ballot box. Such a triumph would have made a mockery of sixty years of Afrikaner determination to avoid British domination: the heroic endeavours of the Great Trek, the establishment of the new republics, the smashing victories of the Transvaal War of 1880–81, would all have been in vain. Kruger put his feelings plainly when he said of the Uitlanders on one occasion, 'Their rights! Yes, they'll get them over my dead body.' And on another, 'I will not hand my country over to strangers.'

Kruger's denial of full civil rights to the Uitlanders was not in itself a cause of the Boer War, but it did present the British government with the moral justification for pushing the Transvaal to the

The Boer Estimate of THE BRITISH LION (NOBLE ANIMAL) IN SOUTH AFRICA 1881

brink of hostilities. The Conservative and Unionist government elected in 1895 proved especially susceptible to the Uitlander predicament. There was, of course, an important principle involved: that of the protection of British citizens overseas. But more than that, the new Colonial Secretary, Joseph Chamberlain, came to believe that it was essential to extend British influence throughout southern Africa, from the Cape to the Zambezi and beyond. Chamberlain possessed an essentially businesslike view of the Empire and of British interests; a successful Birmingham businessman himself, he sought to exploit, even corner, colonial markets and raw materials. The Transvaal with its expanding economy was a choice and tempting plum. Furthermore, it became increasingly likely that, as it grew in wealth and standing, the Transvaal would come to dominate South Africa; any future federation might well be under the republic's Vierkleur rather than the Union Jack.

Cecil Rhodes, within South Africa, had become convinced

The British Lion flees back to Natal after the disastrous defeats of 1881 during the first Boer War.

17

by 1895 that the Transvaal government must be overthrown – by force if necessary. Rhodes was the Empire's standard-bearer against Kruger. Nicknamed 'the Colossus', Rhodes was an essentially curious figure, squeaky-voiced, assertive, and abnormally fearful of women. Yet he had built up substantial interests in the Rand gold industry, had founded his own colonies in north and southern Rhodesia, north of the Limpopo River, and had become prime minister of the self-governing Cape Colony in 1890. He put his millions to work in the cause of both the British Empire and his own grandiose fantasies. His own company, the British South Africa Company, had opened up the Rhodesias; his private army, the police force of the British South Africa Company, had crushed the Mashona and the Matabele; his armed paddle-steamers plied the Zambezi. 'What, Mr Rhodes,' Queen Victoria once asked, 'have you been doing since last we met?' Rhodes allegedly replied, 'Merely adding two provinces to Your Majesty's dominions.'

Rhodes attempted to overthrow Kruger's republic in December 1895 by an armed raid launched from the Pitsani strip recently acquired from Bechuanaland. The invasion of the Transvaal was to be led by his old friend and lieutenant from his Kimberley mining days, Dr Leander Starr Jameson. But the Jameson Raid was a disastrous flop. The Uitlanders of Johannesburg were meant to rise in rebellion and link up with Jameson's troopers, drawn from the Rhodesian-based British South African police force. The British High Commissioner for South Africa and Governor of the Cape, Sir Hercules Robinson, would then have stepped in as mediator.

The plan went wrong. The Uitlander uprising was a half-hearted affair, confirming some British statesmen in their view that Mammon not Queen Victoria was the true idol of Johannesburg. Jameson's invasion force was routed, quickly rounded up by Afrikaner commandos, and handed over to the British authorities for trial. The raid ruined Rhodes's standing in Cape politics, and he was obliged to resign his premiership. Kruger's reputation, however, was boosted by the humiliating failure of the raid, and the German Kaiser Wilhelm II sent him a telegram of strident congratulation. Apart from the Kaiser, Afrikaners throughout South Africa rallied to Kruger: moderate, anti-Krugerite opinion in the Transvaal was temporarily silenced; the Orange Free State looked more benignly upon its northern sister republic; in the Cape, the Afrikaners, who accounted for two thirds of the white population, felt more strongly than ever their ties of kinship with the Afrikaners of the republics – and Jan Hofmeyr's Afrikaner Bond party brought

Opposite The Colossus steps out. A cartoon of 1897 shows Cecil Rhodes persuing his dream of a Cape-to-Cairo link-up of British power.

19

down Rhodes's premiership by withdrawing its support in the Cape parliament. The British Colonial Secretary, Joseph Chamberlain, was suspected of collusion in the planning of the Jameson Raid, though the Committee of Enquiry whitewashed him of complicity.

All in all, British policy in South Africa had suffered a prodigious setback. Within four years, however, Chamberlain had regained the initiative. The Transvaal was isolated by a series of diplomatic manoeuvres, of which the most spectacular was the Anglo-German agreement of 1898. This agreement, which concerned a share-out of Portugal's colonies of Mozambique and Angola in the event of the almost bankrupt Portuguese government having to mortgage them, involved Germany's diplomatic abandonment of the Transvaal. The German ambassador in London, Hatzfeldt, said plainly that the arrangement 'would be a public advertisement to the Transvaal government that they had nothing more to hope for from Germany, or indeed from any European power'.

So that Britain's case in South Africa should be put with the utmost effectiveness, the government appointed a new High Commissioner and Governor of the Cape in 1897. This was Sir Alfred Milner, ex-scholar of Balliol, ex-Treasury Civil Servant, arch-administrator and confirmed race-patriot. Though not at the outset averse to mediation between British and Afrikaner interests, within a year Milner had come to the conclusion that war with the Transvaal was highly likely, if not inevitable.

There followed a well orchestrated exercise in late-nineteenth century brinkmanship. The Uitlanders were presented to the British public, and world opinion, as a worthy and unjustly persecuted group. Petitions to Queen Victoria were sent from Johannesburg, and Milner officially referred to the Uitlanders as 'helots' – the slaves of Ancient Greece. In May 1899, Milner and Kruger met at Bloemfontein to try and negotiate a settlement of the Uitlander problem. The conference predictably failed: Kruger made concessions which the British side considered inadequate, and the meeting broke up, having created the impression in the United Kingdom that Kruger was not prepared to make reasonable sacrifices.

In Britain the public had thus been prepared for a war to 'free' the Uitlanders. In the Sudan, Kitchener's brilliant campaign of conquest was drawing to a successful conclusion, thus making possible a full-scale military concentration upon South Africa. As early as June 1899 Chamberlain and Milner had discussed the question of troop reinforcements; in August there were further warlike preparations; by the beginning of October there were nearly twenty

thousand Imperial troops in the Cape and Natal, and when fighting actually broke out on 12 October there were seventy thousand British soldiers either in South Africa or on the high seas.

The British government completed their diplomatic campaign by manoeuvring the Transvaal into issuing a warlike ultimatum on 9 October. The ultimatum demanded the withdrawal of all British troops on the Transvaal's frontiers and that those on their way to South Africa should be sent back. On 3 October the first of the British reinforcements had landed at Durban. The spring grass was up – vital forage for the horses of the Boer commandos. The British government rejected the Transvaal's ultimatum, the Orange Free State rallied to Kruger's side, and the great Boer War of 1899–1902 began on 12 October.

Opposite Sir Alfred Milner, Governor of the Cape and High Commissioner for South Africa, 1898–1905 and, with Chamberlain, one of the architects of the war.

Chapter 2

Briton and Boer:
The Opposing Forces

The opposing sides were apparently ludicrously unequal. The British Empire, within whose borders dwelt almost a quarter of the human race, was at war with two sparsely populated republics in South Africa. Britain was still, arguably, the greatest power in the world, her navy invincible and ubiquitous, her overseas trade colossal, her global influence all-pervasive. She controlled the Cape, Natal, the Rhodesias and Bechuanaland, all pressing upon the Boer republics' frontiers; the Uitlanders were a fifth column within the Transvaal, and by no means all Afrikaners were spoiling for so impossible a fight. In the end, Britain put 448,000 troops into the field; the Boers could at no time call upon more than seventy thousand men, and probably never had more than forty thousand in active service. Moreover, the Afrikaner forces were almost exclusively composed of civilians under arms.

The war certainly looked as if it would be over by Christmas. In Britain the mood was initially one of exhilaration as the khaki-clad infantry marched to the troopships, as the Admiralty hastily mustered 600,000 tons of shipping for the men, horses and guns of the Army Corps dispatched to South Africa, as General Sir Redvers Buller, VC, left Waterloo Station for embarkation at Southampton and the command of Her Majesty's forces in the campaign. Rudyard Kipling, bard of Empire, wrote stirringly:

When you've shouted 'Rule Britannia', when you've sung 'God Save
    the Queen',
    When you've finished killing Kruger with your mouth,
Will you kindly drop a shilling in my little tambourine
    For a gentleman in Khaki ordered South?
He's an absent-minded beggar, and his weaknesses are great –
    But we and Paul must take him as we find him –
He is out on active service, wiping something off a slate –
    And he's left a lot of little things behind him!
Duke's son – cook's son – son of a hundred Kings –
    (Fifty thousand horse and foot going to Table Bay!)
Each of 'em doing his country's work
    (and who's to look after their things?)
Pass the hat for your credit's sake,
    and pay – pay – pay!

Opposite British troops (and wagons) entrained for the front, 1900.

The dispatch of an army corps of fifty thousand revealed serious inadequacies in the British military establishment. For one thing, home defences had to be pared to the bone. So serious was the depletion of forces stationed in Britain that the War Office immediately 25

pressed the Cabinet to approve a policy of 'replacement', which
involved the embodiment of a number of militia battalions and the
issuing of contracts for new uniforms and supplies. George
Wyndham, Under-Secretary at the War Office, told Arthur
Balfour, First Lord of the Treasury, in October 1899, that unless
'replacement' was speedily effected the home army would be left
without 'personnel and material' for adequate action or for training
recruits, there would only be eight cavalry regiments left in the
United Kingdom (not enough for home defence or for supplying
the Indian Army in the coming year), and Britain would be 'left
with nothing but four gun batteries'.

The British forces, despite their numerical advantage in South
Africa, had scarcely profited from their humiliations during the brief
war of 1880–81. The average infantryman was still expected to obey
rigid instructions to the last syllable, to keep splendid order, and to
let his superiors do the thinking for him, whereas each Afrikaner
was his own general. The British army possessed no general staff to

plan and co-ordinate tactics and strategy, and a paltry £11,000 was spent per annum on maintaining the Intelligence Division. The 'ideal British battle' was still one like the engagement at Omdurman in 1898, when the spear-waving Dervishes of the Sudan ran in their thousands against their opponents' Maxim guns and rifles and were annihilated; Kitchener, the victor of Omdurman, was later to complain in South Africa that the Boers would not 'stand up to a fair fight'.

The British army had not properly understood the importance of mounted infantry. Ten per cent of the Imperial troops were admittedly mounted, but these were mainly cavalry who, although they carried the new-fangled carbines as well as sabres and lances, remained cavalrymen – not mounted infantry. The authorities were soon searching the Empire for mounted men. Happily the self-governing colonies were able to plug an important gap or two: 1,000 expert horsemen were raised in Canada, the New South Wales Lancers played a conspicuous part in the war, and from southern Africa itself came the Imperial Light Horse (mostly recruited from the Uitlanders of Johannesburg), the Natal Mounted Volunteers, the Cape Police, the Kimberley Light Horse, and several other units.

These valuable contributions were only part of the generous colonial response to the war, and eventually fifty-five thousand men, mostly from the self-governing parts of the Empire, served in South Africa – nearly double the number of the British expeditionary force sent to the Crimea in 1854. Even so, the bulk of the colonial troops did not arrive until the war was well under way, and it was not until the beginning of 1901 that Lord Kitchener managed to assemble sufficiently large numbers of mounted men to try to cope with Boer mobility. Despite the eighty thousand mounted troops under British command by 1901, however, their quality remained variable, and few units could match the Afrikaners in versatility and guile. One important source of manpower, moreover, was denied to the British in South Africa. This was the Indian Army, composed of over 200,000 fine troops, of which some 150,000 were native Indians. In view of Afrikaner attitudes towards non-Europeans, the British government was tactful enough not to put Sikhs, Punjabis or Madrasis into the field against them; after all, peace would one day have to be made with the Boers. There was, however, a volunteer Indian ambulance unit led by a young lawyer named Gandhi, who had already achieved a measure of fame through his campaign to win adequate civil rights for the Indians of Natal.

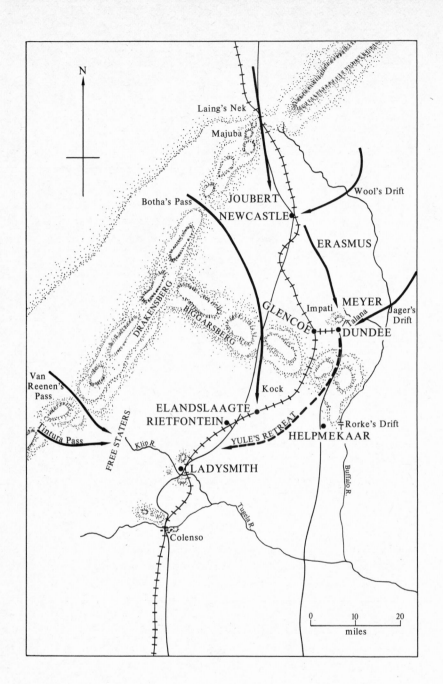

N

Laing's Nek

Majuba

Botha's Pass

JOUBERT

NEWCASTLE

Wool's Drift

ERASMUS

MEYER

Impati

Jager's
Drift

GLENCOE

DRAKENSBERG

BIGGARSBERG

Talana

DUNDEE

Van
Reenen's
Pass

Kock

ELANDSLAAGTE

RIETFONTEIN

Rorke's Drift

FREE STATERS

Tintura Pass

Klip R.

YULE'S RETREAT

HELPMEKAAR

LADYSMITH

Buffalo R.

Tugela R.

Colenso

0   10   20

miles

28   The Boer invasion route into Natal, October 1889.

The bulk of the British forces used in the Boer War were regular soldiers. In contrast the Afrikaner armies contained few regular troops: there were less than two thousand men drawn from various police detachments, and a few hundred artillerymen from the Transvaal's Staatsartillerie and from the Free State's artillery corps, which was Prussian-trained and even wore Prussian helmets. Their guns were excellent – from the 94-pounder 'Long Toms' to the 1-pounder Vickers-Maxim pom-poms, and the 75 mm Krupp and Creusot quick-firing field pieces. In all, however, they possessed no more than seventy guns, whereas the British forces eventually built up a vast preponderance of artillery and could count on a thousand 15-pounders alone, as well as on nearly a thousand machine guns.

Of course, the crucial test came when both sides handled their artillery. Here the Boers often showed greater ingenuity and skill. When they opened up on Ladysmith with their 'Long Toms', Joseph Chamberlain remarked irritably that Lord Lansdowne, Secretary of State for War, had told him 'that modern guns require elaborate platforms and mountings which took a year to consolidate. The Boers apparently find no difficulty in working their 'Long Toms' without these elaborate precautions. On the whole I am terribly afraid that our War Office is as inefficient as usual.'

Much the same comparisons can be made between the small arms used by both sides: the Afrikaners were mostly equipped with the clip-loading Mauser rifle; the British carried the Lee-Enfield rifle whose magazine had to be loaded round by round. Neither rifle was obviously superior in range to the other, but given Afrikaner marksmanship and expertise the Mauser, with its quick loading action, was generally employed far more effectively than the Lee-Enfield.

The deficiencies in British training and tactics were soon to be evident to all. On 16 December 1899 the brother of the Duke of Portland, who was serving in South Africa, wrote home angrily, 'the Boers have much longer range guns and rifles than us which is a great handicap to us and a gross mistake by the War Office'. He went on to complain that British troops could not get near enough to shell the Boers out of their positions, and asked for a good telescope as his field glasses were not strong enough to search out the Afrikaners.

The creator of Sherlock Holmes, Arthur Conan Doyle, who was the doctor in charge of the Bloemfontein Military Hospital (after the town's capture), wrote a penetrating analysis of British inadequacies in his book *The Great Boer War*:

Transvaal Boers off to the war. Note their commandeered transport and its English-language advertisements.

It costs as much to convey and feed a worthless man as a good one. If he
is not a dead shot with a rifle, what is the use of carrying him seven
thousand miles in order to place him in a firing line? One man who hits
his mark outweighs ten who miss it, and only asks one-tenth of the food
and transport. If by paying three times as much we can secure that one
man, it is an obvious economy to the country to do so.

So much for the men themselves, but it is in their training that there
is the room for criticism. The idea that an infantry soldier is a pikeman
has never quite departed in our army. He is still to march in step as the
pikeman did, to go steadily shoulder to shoulder, to rush forward with
his pike advanced. All this is mediaeval and dangerous. There is only
one thing which wins a modern battle, and that is straight shooting. To
hit your enemy and to avoid being hit yourself are the two points of the
game, and the one is as important as the other …

The taking of cover, the most important of all infantry exercises,
appears to be even more neglected than our musketry …

Entrenching also is one of the weak points of our infantry. As Mr
Bennet Burleigh has observed, the sappers have a bad influence upon the
infantry, for they teach the foot soldier that he will have things done for
him which he should be able to do for himself. Every infantry officer
should know how to plan trenches, and every infantry soldier how to
make them … Sometimes they were even ludicrous, like some which I
saw myself – in a position which might well have been attacked –
where the sides of the loopholes in the parapet were made of empty jam
pots …

Passing on to the cavalry, we come to the branch of the service which

A British 15-pounder being pulled by oxen.

appears to me to be the most in need of reform … Lances, swords, and revolvers have only one place – the museum. How many times was the lance or the sword fleshed in this war, and how many men did we lose in the attempts, and how many tons of useless metal have our over-burdened horses carried about the country?

The very great advantage which the Boers possessed – one which enabled half a dozen Boer guns to hold as many British batteries – was that their cannon were as invisible as their rifles. The first use which a Boer makes of his guns is to conceal them. The first use which a British major makes of his is to expose them in a straight line with correct interspaces, each gun so near its neighbour that a lucky shell dropping between them might cripple the crews of each.

Conan Doyle was not the only distinguished man of letters to see the war at first hand. Rudyard Kipling came out to edit the *Friend*, a newspaper for soldiers, published in Bloemfontein. He had no doubt as to what the war was about, and wrote trenchantly, 'It is only the Little Englanders in London who say that the Transvaal is merely fighting for its independence. Out here, both sides realize it is a question of which race runs the country.' Edgar Wallace, soon to become famous for his detective stories, was a war correspondent for the *Daily Mail*. Then there was the young Winston Churchill, a war correspondent for the *Morning Post*, who was captured after a train ambush in Natal; he subsequently escaped and the Boers

33

offered a £25 reward for his recapture, describing him as of 'in-different build, pale appearance, reddish brown hair, a small moustache, scarcely perceptible, who cannot pronounce the letter "S" properly'.

Although the Boers could not boast a Conan Doyle or a Winston Churchill, a number of men who had some claim to fame fought on their side in the two thousand strong Foreign Legion. There was an Irish contingent of some two hundred men, which included John McBride, later to be executed as one of the leaders of the 1916 Dublin Easter uprising. Among the German volunteers was a relative of the airship designer von Zeppelin. A French count and a Russian colonel were also leaders of various volunteer units.

But the ranks of the Boer armies were overwhelmingly composed of Afrikaner burghers: 32,000 from the Transvaal, 23,000 from the Orange Free State and perhaps 10,000 'rebels' from the Cape, as well as 2,700 regular soldiers. Boer males were called up into the commando units which existed even in peacetime. One Free Stater, Victor Pohl, later recalled the mustering of one such force:

> Soon there were gathered a large number of farmer-soldiers, hefty, clear-eyed, bronzed, and good-natured men from the open veld … Sitting their horses like cowboys, they wore what they had stood in when they were called up, and their rifles and bandoliers were slung carelessly on their persons according to individual inclination. A raincoat or blanket, or both, were rolled tightly and fastened to the pommel or tail of each saddle, and in most cases saddle-bags stuffed to bursting with boar-rusks, bread, and biltong [dried raw meat], completed their outfits. To an outsider this motley and unwarlike gathering would have appeared to be without leaders or discipline, for the Boer leaders did not differ in appearance from the rest of the slouching burghers. And yet when they addressed the men they were listened to with earnest attention, although not with parade-ground rigidity. What these men lacked in military discipline was largely made up for by their independence of thought and action, and their sense of responsibility. Moreover many of the men were deeply religious, and all these qualities, combined with their profound faith in their cause, their reliance on themselves and their Mausers, and the knowledge that they were fighting for their homes and country, made of this undisciplined crowd a formidable army, one to whose prowess the civilized world was to pay tribute.

Each Boer army was led by a commandant-general; under him were field-generals, then commandants, who in turn had field-cornets under them; finally there were the corporals, who each commanded between ten and seventy men. Because they were composed overwhelmingly of civilians, the Boer forces had an easy-going, democratic organization: for example, the field-cornets and

The war correspondent
Winston Churchill
(scowling, far right) as a
prisoner of the Boers.

corporals were elected by the men. There were some disadvantages
in the democratic character of the Boer forces: for instance, they
still thought of themselves as civilians under arms, and took leave or
slipped off home whenever they chose; they were also apt to melt
away when the going got particularly tough, for 'dying in the last
ditch' was no part of their philosophy, which was better expressed
in an Afrikaner saying first given currency during the Transvaal
War of 1880–81: 'You English fight to die; we Boers fight to live'.

Individual Boer generals had to keep their men together through
military success or by personal persuasion. The sort of problem that
Afrikaner generals had to face was neatly illustrated early in the war
when Free State Commandant-General Prinsloo had to telephone
General Botha (of the Transvaal) to inform him that his officers
were attending a cattle sale on the day fixed for the attack on
Elandslaagte and would therefore not be available for the battle.

Overall, however, the individual initiative and sense of responsibility of the Boer troops more than compensated for their bouts of
erratic behaviour. They were excellent horsemen, and thus able to
reconnoitre superbly and to cover large distances quickly, whether
in retreat or advance. Their use of cover was exemplary, and the
smokeless powder of their rifle cartridges and artillery shells enabled

35

The redoubtable
Afrikaner general Koos
de la Rey.

them to conceal their positions even more effectively. Boer marksmanship was legendary, and was maintained even when they
opened rapid fire. They were also at one with the terrain, and able
to use it with a sure touch. Above all, they were fighting to preserve
their way of life, their homesteads and their families. Many of them
equated British rule with social revolution, as Winston Churchill
found when one of his Boer captors said, 'We want to be left alone.
We are free, you are not free'. When asked what he meant, the
Afrikaner went on, 'Well, is it right that a dirty Kaffir should walk
on the pavement – without a pass too? This is what they do in your
British Colonies. Brother! Equal! Ugh! Free! Not a bit! We know
how to treat Kaffirs.'

The Boer generals in the field were of variable quality, and were
often chosen because of their successes in the 1880–81 war or in
conflicts with the Bantu. In 1899 a good number of them were of
advanced years: Piet Cronje was sixty-four, General Joubert sixty-
eight, and General Johannes Kock, who led his men in a frock coat
and a top hat, sixty-four. But as the war progressed, younger men
came to the fore, especially during the lengthy and gruelling period
of guerilla warfare. Among these commanders were soldiers who

36

would soon gain international reputations, men like Louis Botha, Jan Christiaan Smuts, Christiaan de Wet, Koos de la Rey, J. B. Hertzog, and Henrik Beyers.

Still, at the outset of the war, there seemed no reason why such amateurs, even though talented, should stand in the way of the Empire's professional soldiers. A popular marching song 'Goodbye Dolly Gray' swept the music halls in Britain, and patriots assumed it to be merely the overture to inevitable military conquest. Moreover there was unbounded public confidence in the South African Commander-in-Chief, General Buller: 'farver' said the urchin in the cartoon, ''as gawn to South Africa, and tooken 'is strap!'

But Buller's real capacities fell far short of appearances. Come to that, even Dolly Gray was a second-hand trollop who had waved American troops off to the war against Spain the year before! Buller's failings, however, were to prove rather more serious. He was sixty-years-old in 1899, overweight, ponderous and self-indulgent; he later boasted that he consumed a pint of good champagne every day during his campaigning in South Africa – and there was certainly a good deal of evidence that his judgement had been impaired by heavy drinking. Equally serious, though unavoidable, was his complete lack of experience against European opponents; when he left for South Africa he had never commanded more than two thousand men at once, and even then against a variety of poorly armed indigenous people. He was undoubtedly brave, and had won the Victoria Cross at Hlobane during the Zulu War; he also took remarkable care of his soldiers' welfare. Yet beneath the surface glitter he was painfully unsure of himself, and was soon to reveal considerable prowess as a military fumbler and ditherer, thus amply justifying a brother officer's description of him as 'a superb Major, a mediocre Colonel and an abysmally poor General'.

Nonetheless, there seemed no reason why Buller and the Army Corps that were descending upon South Africa should not achieve prompt victory. The British forces would move north along the railway lines from Port Elizabeth, Cape Town and East London, and would eventually sweep on to the Afrikaner capitals of Bloemfontein, in the Orange Free State, and Pretoria, in the Transvaal. The plan seemed perfectly adequate, and as the *Dunottar Castle*, with Buller and his staff aboard, left Southampton there seemed every justification for the enthusiasm of a big, red-faced onlooker who repeatedly shouted 'Remember Majuba!' 'He need not have worried,' a member of Buller's staff was later to recall, 'we soon had plenty of Majubas of our own.'

Chapter 3

The First Battles, October 1899

E ven as Buller steamed towards the Cape, British forces in South Africa were suffering sharp reverses. Far from waiting like bemused rabbits to be devoured by their ponderous enemies, the Boers immediately struck against Cape Colony and Natal. Three Afrikaner columns invaded Natal, the soft under-belly of British power: Utrecht, Dundee and Newcastle were occupied, and soon Ladysmith, on the junction of the railway lines between Natal, the Free State and the Transvaal, was under siege. Meanwhile, further west, Afrikaner troops invested two more towns that lay on the vital railway line that ran from the important junction at De Aar, in the Cape, roughly parallel with the western borders of the Free State and the Transvaal until it finally entered the British protectorate of Bechuanaland. The name of Kimberley was already world-famous, that of Mafeking was about to become so. To the south of the Free State's border with Cape Colony, Boer columns also pushed towards the railway junction of Stormberg and towards the rail link between Naauwpoort and De Aar.

A young girl of Russian parentage, Freda Schlosberg, recorded the excitement of these early days of the war in a journal she kept at her select boarding school in Pretoria:

> Newcastle has been occupied by the Boers. The news brings great rejoicing. Mafeking and Kimberley are besieged, and Ladysmith is threatened.
> 'Victory follows victory.' 'The English are being driven into the sea.' 'Boer arms are successful everywhere.' The Transvaal is very gay. The Hollanders, Irish and Germans are celebrating. 'The Boers will soon be masters of South Africa.'

Boer strategy was based on the belief – a belief to be amply justified by events – that time was not on their side. They hoped, therefore, to achieve such striking early successes that the British would become disheartened and negotiate a settlement, just as had happened after General Colley's defeat at Majuba Hill in 1881. A string of early victories, moreover, would encourage the Cape Dutch to flock to the republics' standards, and would rally international opinion against the oppressions of John Bull.

The first engagements of the war came in north Natal. Here British forces consisted of a brigade of four thousand men under General Sir William Symons at Dundee, and eight thousand men at Ladysmith under the veteran Sir George White, VC. Boer columns were pressing towards Ladysmith from the north (Transvaal

Opposite 'A Chip off the Old Block'. Charge of the Fifth Lancers at the Battle of Elandslaagte.

39

commandos crossing the Drakensberg range at Botha's Pass and Laing's Nek) and from the west (where Free Staters began to move through Van Reenen's Pass and Tintura Pass). Newcastle, to the north of Dundee and Ladysmith, was occupied without a fight. General White almost immediately gave a demonstration of that wavering indecisiveness that was to lead to such embarrassment for British arms in Natal. At first he ordered Symons to retire and join him in Ladysmith; Symons declined to do so, and White finally let him have his way.

At 2.30 a.m. on 20 October the first battle of the war, Talana, began when Lukas Meyer's scouts clashed with a British picket of the Royal Dublin Fusiliers at Smith's Nek, the pass running between Talana Hill and Lennox Hill, to the east of Dundee. General Symons, on hearing this news, concluded that it was merely a raid, and of no great significance.

When the morning mist cleared at 5.30 a.m., however, the British troops positioned on the partly dried up bed of Sand Spruit saw to their dismay that the crests of both Talana Hill and Lennox Hill were thick with Afrikaners. Within seconds Boer gunners fired the first shell of the war over the heads of the British troops.

Symons immediately ordered his infantry to join the Dublin Fusiliers, the mounted infantry of the 60th, the 18th Hussars and some field batteries at Sand Spruit. The 13th, 67th and 69th Field Batteries eventually opened fire upon the Boers on Talana. So effective was their bombardment that the Boer guns were silenced, and over a thousand commandos panicked, leapt onto their horses, and made off. The bulk of the Afrikaner forces, however, stayed, concealed among the boulders upon the summit.

General Symons now prepared to drive the enemy off Talana by a frontal attack backed by artillery fire. By about 7.30 a.m. units of the Royal Dublin Fusiliers, the Royal Irish Fusiliers, and the 60th Foot Regiment had taken cover in a plantation of eucalyptus trees between Sand Spruit and Talana Hill. The Dublin Fusiliers soon moved northwards out of the wood, but they were raked by such crippling fire that they were virtually knocked out of the battle.

It was left to the 60th and the Irish Fusiliers to mount the frontal attack on Talana Hill, supported by the 69th and 13th Field Batteries. For some time, however, nothing happened, and General Symons rode into the eucalyptus wood to see what was holding up the advance. He dismounted and walked among the men shouting 'Push on', and other words of encouragement. Several walls ran along the edge of the wood and on the slopes of Talana, and Symons stepped through a gap in one of them and was almost immediately

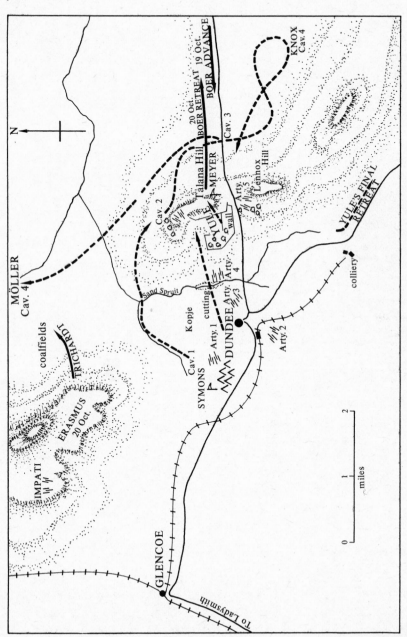

The Battle of Talana,
20 October 1899.

41

shot in the stomach. Though his wound proved to be fatal, he coolly instructed General Yule, the artillery commander, to press the attack, and then rode back to the field dressing station, where he subsequently died.

Even as General Symons's life was slipping from him, the men of the 60th and the Irish Fusiliers were fighting their way doggedly up the slopes of Talana, using the various walls for cover where possible. Despite a hail of accurate fire from the Boers' Mausers, the men made a final assault on the summit, driving off many of their foes with the bayonet. As the British troops made for the summit, however, their own artillery, hampered by the now poor light, brought down a heavy fire on both attackers and defenders alike. Once this terrible error was rectified, the British line was able to surge forward again, and found that the Boers had deserted the summit of Talana. The Afrikaners on Lennox Hill also withdrew.

In the confusion of the Boer retreat, the British artillery, shocked at having only recently fired on their own men, failed to punish the enemy as they withdrew to the east. Nor did the cavalry cut them off, for Colonel Möller, with the men of the 18th Hussars and some mounted infantry of the 60th, got himself trapped by a Boer commando unit at Adelaide Farm some four miles to the north of Talana Hill. By 4 p.m. Möller was forced to surrender, together with nine officers and 205 men; eight of these troopers had been killed and twenty-three wounded.

In all, the British lost some five hundred men, including killed, wounded and prisoners. The Boers lost 150. It was a Pyrrhic victory for the British – indeed in a sense a defeat, for General Yule soon decided to move his forces back to Ladysmith, leaving Dundee open to enemy occupation.

Meanwhile, some twenty-five miles to the south-west old General Kock's troops were advancing on Elandslaagte, half-way between Dundee and Ladysmith. Indeed, on 19 October, advanced units of Kock's men took Elandslaagte station and its environs, completely cutting rail, road and telegraphic communications between Dundee and Ladysmith. By 20 October Kock's main force reached Elandslaagte. That evening the Boers held a concert in the hotel near the railway station; some British prisoners from a captured supply train were invited, and both 'God Save the Queen' and the Transvaal's anthem 'Volkslied' were sung vociferously at the concert.

The next day the Battle of Elandslaagte took place, when General Sir John French moved north from Ladysmith to clear the path for General Yule's forces retreating after the Battle of Talana.

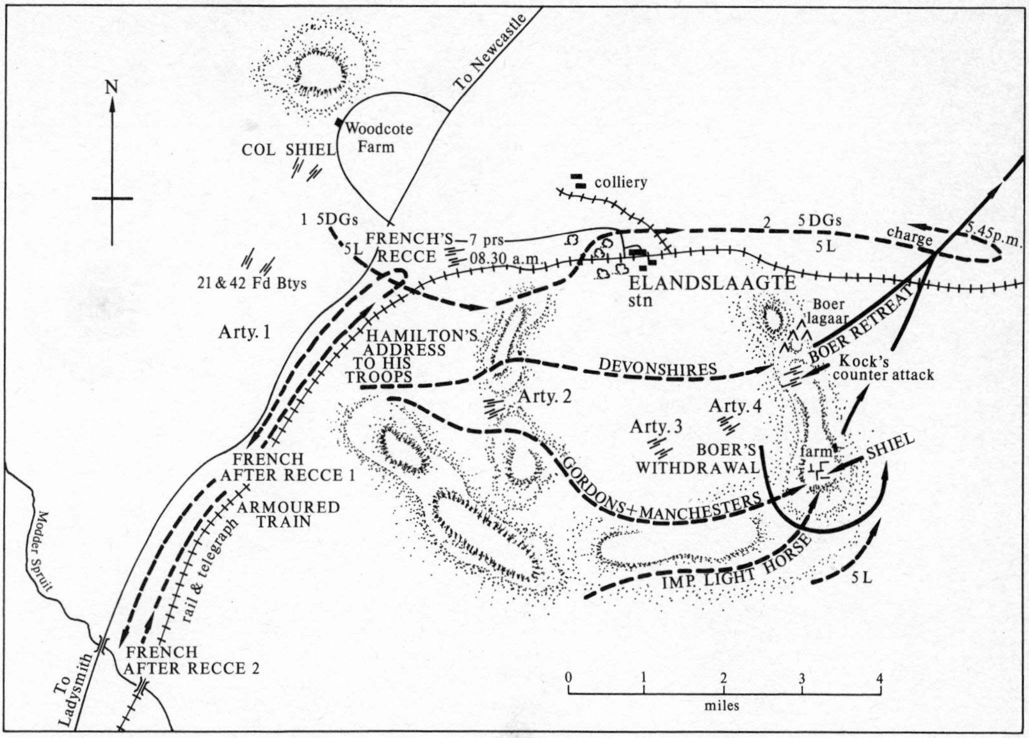
N
To Newcastle
Woodcote Farm
COL SHIEL
colliery
1 5DGs
5L
FRENCH'S RECCE
7 prs
08.30 a.m.
21 & 42 Fd Btys
2
5DGs
5L
charge
5.45p.m.
ELANDSLAAGTE stn
Boer lagaar
BOER RETREAT
Arty. 1
HAMILTON'S ADDRESS TO HIS TROOPS
DEVONSHIRES
Kock's counter attack
Arty. 2
Arty. 4
Arty. 3
BOER'S WITHDRAWAL
farm
SHIEL
FRENCH AFTER RECCE 1
ARMOURED TRAIN
GORDONS+MANCHESTERS
Modder Spruit
rail & telegraph
IMP. LIGHT HORSE
5L
FRENCH AFTER RECCE 2
To Ladysmith
0
1
2
3
4
miles

The Battle of Elandslaagte, 21 October 1899.

French's patrols made contact with the Afrikaners holding the station, and the Natal Volunteer Field Battery cleared both friend and foe out of the station buildings with fire from their 7-pounder guns. But the Boers on the kopjes to the south-east in turn shelled the 7-pounders, causing French to fall back to where the Modder Spruit crossed both the railway to Elandslaagte and the road north to Newcastle.

When the reinforcements for which French had telegraphed Ladysmith had arrived, the main battle began. Sir John had squadrons of the Imperial Light Horse, the 5th Dragoon Guards and the 5th Lancers; besides the 7-pounders, he had some 15-pounders of the 21st and 42nd Field Batteries; half a battalion of the 1st Manchesters arrived, followed by seven companies of the 1st Battalion of the Devonshires and five companies of the 2nd Battalion of the Gordon Highlanders.

French advanced up the Newcastle road, delaying his main attack until three o'clock in the afternoon, when all the reinforcements had arrived. The battle area was south of Elandslaagte station, and consisted of a plain ringed round by a horseshoe of hills, with the opening of the horseshoe in the north; the Boer laager was near the top of the eastern side of the hill formation. The

Gordon Highlanders
standing by their
heliographs – devices
for sending messages by
reflecting the rays of the
sun.

commander of the infantry, Colonel Ian Hamilton, a survivor of
Majuba Hill, and much favoured by General White, addressed his
men in stirring words, telling them that they would throw the
Boers off the hills before sunset, and that London newsboys would
be shouting the news of their victory the next day. The infantrymen
cheered lustily, shouting out, 'We'll do it, sir! We'll do it!'

At first the attack went well. Sir George White arrived from Ladysmith, with an escort of Natal Mounted Rifles, to watch the progress
of the battle. A huge thunderstorm closed in upon the battle area,
however, thus cutting down visibility. Since the daylight was also
beginning to fade, French ordered Hamilton's infantry to advance
after the Boer positions had been shelled for a mere half-hour. The
44 Afrikaners were easily dislodged from the western side of the horse-

shoe of hills, but the eastern side – including a formidable hogsback – was to prove a more difficult objective.

Nonetheless, the Devonshires, advancing across the plain towards the hogsback, made good progress due to their open formation – a lesson Hamilton had learnt the hard way during the Majuba campaign. But twelve hundred yards from the Boer positions, they were halted by heavy and accurate rifle fire.

The Manchesters and the Gordons had meanwhile cut round the inside bend of the horseshoe; they were accompanied on foot by Uitlanders of the Imperial Light Horse, who moved along the bend of the horseshoe, to their right.

The assault on the southern flank of the hogsback was a difficult one, rendered doubly hazardous by the thunderstorm breaking and drastically reducing visibility. When at last the rain eased off, the infantry began to climb the rock-strewn slope, towards the barbed wire fences protecting the Afrikaners. Many British troops were shot down, especially when they bunched together to cut paths through the wire. The men of the Imperial Light Horse, having virtually annihilated a force of Germans under a General Schiel, were in turn decimated; half of the Gordons' officers were out of action, and the Manchesters cut to pieces.

Colonel Hamilton then decided to order the Devonshires to resume their advance. The bugles of the approaching Devonshires put new heart into the other battered infantry units and, fixing bayonets, they swept the Boers from the hogsback, capturing two guns in the process.

But the infantry's triumph was short-lived. Seeing some Boers in the laager waving white flags, Hamilton ordered a ceasefire. The ceasefire was rudely interrupted, however, when about forty men under old General Kock, in his frock coat and top hat, suddenly appeared below the crest of the hogsback and blazed away at the British troops. Driven from the summit, the infantry were rallied by Hamilton and by French himself; joined by the Devonshires, they once more hurled the enemy off the heights, the Gordons shouting 'Remember Majuba!'

Overleaf A quick kip. British troops rest amid boots and saddles.

As the Boers mounted their horses and streamed away from the hills, the 5th Dragoon Guards and the 5th Lancers charged upon them in the dusk. The Afrikaners were sabred down, and speared by the British lances (two unfortunates on one pony were stuck through by the same lance). The cavalrymen wrought havoc among the Boers, until darkness called a halt to their activities.

Elandslaagte was a clear-cut British victory. The Boers had been driven from their chosen positions by a good co-operative effort on

45

the part of artillery, cavalry and infantry, and three VCs were gained by British soldiers. Though infantry losses had been heavy in the final stages of the assault, the news of the victory was encouraging for the British, and Freda Schlosberg recorded on 21 October that:

> The English language paper, *Standard and Digger News*, which arrives by post from Johannesburg, reports that 'General French shelled strongly entrenched Boer forces at Elandslaagte, fifteen miles north of Ladysmith and after a bayonet attack put them to flight. General Kock was wounded and he and three hundred of his men, and General Schiel, commander of the German Corps, was taken prisoner. Boer officials in Pretoria are reported to be uneasy and hospitals are preparing to receive the wounded.'

General Kock was indeed mortally wounded, and died in Ladysmith. General French's reputation was boosted by the encounter, and proved to be durable enough to survive the later tribulations of the war.

Despite Elandslaagte, however, the prospects for British arms in north Natal remained bleak. Columns of Transvaalers and Free Staters continued to close in upon the forces around Ladysmith. General Yule, retreating south from Dundee towards Ladysmith, made a bold detour, over rain-drenched hills and through dangerously high rivers, away from the main road. Eventually, exhausted, they reached Ladysmith, to the cheers of the garrison.

Yule's retreating column had passed close to Rietfontein, between Elandslaagte and Ladysmith. Here, on 24 October, five thousand British troops had held off the Free State commandos, led by General Erasmus, who had just occupied and looted Dundee. Once the British force learnt that Yule's men had reached Ladysmith, they too pulled back.

On 25 October, Dr Alec Kay, having arrived in Ladysmith as a civil surgeon at the Stationary Hospital, wrote: 'Ladysmith is full of spies. I met one today, a man who had fought against us in the Boer War of 1880 and I knew him to be very bitter towards us. I sent a friend with a message to the Intelligence Department that he had better be arrested; but the reply was, "Ladysmith is so full of spies that one more or less makes no difference."'

Three days later, on 28 October, Dr Kay wrote gloomily, 'The Boers are all around us; the water supply of Ladysmith is cut off. Our war balloons went up and charted the Boer positions.' The siege of Ladysmith had begun.

General White's position was an unenviable one. Cavalry reconnaissance and balloon observations showed that thousands of the enemy were closing in: to the west, Free State commandos, though not apparently making for Ladysmith, were moving down towards Colenso, thus cutting off communications to the south; in the north-west Piet Cronje, in command of units of Free Staters, was situated near Nicholson's Nek and Tchrengula Mountain; to the north, General Erasmus and his men lay between Pepworth Hill and the Modder Spruit; to the east Lukas Meyer's commandos were spread out from the east bank of the Modder Spruit; further round to the north-east were Afrikaners around Long Hill, but these forces were soon withdrawn to a laager east of the Modder Spruit.

In order to break this menacing semi-circle of Boer forces, General White planned to strike northwards with what he called a 're-connaissance in force'; the object was to turn the enemy's east flank on Long Hill, and to close the pass of Nicholson's Nek to reinforcements from the north. White originally planned this counter-manoeuvre for Sunday 29 October, but reconsidered the timing when reminded of the Boers' reluctance to fight on a Sunday. The fateful Battle of Majuba Hill had been forced on the Transvaalers on the sabbath, and afterwards Piet Joubert had remarked scornfully, 'What can you expect from fighting on a Sunday?' A Sunday counter-attack might have stiffened Boer resistance even further. So Monday 30 October was chosen instead. It was no more propitious, and was soon to become known throughout the Empire as 'Mournful Monday'.

At 10.30 a.m. Colonel Carleton led a force of a thousand men out of Ladysmith towards Nicholson's Nek. He had the 1st Battalion of the Gloucesters, the 1st Battalion of the Royal Irish Fusiliers, and the 10th Mountain Battery. They got off to a poor start: the artillery mules were difficult, and subsequently stampeded on the slopes of Tchrengula Mountain, obstinately carrying the mountain guns and a good deal of the spare ammunition back to camp. The clatter, and some nervy firing by some of the troops, alerted the Boers, who began to move against Carleton.

Colonel Grimwood, meanwhile, led out a brigade to bombard and capture Long Hill. He had under his command the 1st and 2nd Battalions of the 60th, the 1st Liverpools, the 1st Leicesters, the 2nd Dublin Fusiliers, the 21st, 42nd and 53rd Field Batteries and the Natal Field Battery.

Colonel Hamilton, confident after his success at Elandslaagte, also left Ladysmith to help in the shelling of Long Hill and then to storm Pepworth Hill with Grimwood's brigade. Hamilton's force

consisted of the 1st Devonshires, the 1st Manchesters, the 2nd Gordon Highlanders and the 13th, 67th and 69th Field Batteries. The cavalry was divided between these two infantry brigades, though Hamilton's troopers were allotted the task of galloping up Bell Spruit and harassing the Boers after they had been swept off the hills.

Colonel Grimwood's approach to Long Hill was little short of disastrous. As they marched under cover of darkness, his artillery units unaccountably left the advancing column and stationed themselves by Flag Hill. The Liverpools, the Dublin Fusiliers, and the mounted infantry units of the Leicesters and the 60th also turned aside at Flag Hill, to the south of Long Hill. Grimwood, knowing nothing of this, plodded on to within a mile of Long Hill and proceeded to launch a dawn attack in accordance with General White's orders. Ian Hamilton's brigade had meanwhile moved to its agreed position south of Pepworth Hill, ready to co-operate with Grimwood's attack.

Grimwood discovered, shortly after dawn, that Long Hill was unoccupied, but his men soon came under enfilading fire from across the Modder Spruit. The brigade commander then sensibly spread his men out, facing east. But where was the cavalry? General French, who had the task of overseeing cavalry manoeuvres, promptly sent in some of his own horsemen and summoned

Hamilton's cavalry as reinforcements. This extended British line, though lacking the units that had dropped by the wayside at Flag Hill, was thus well placed to hold off the Boers from the Modder Spruit area.

Before Pepworth Hill, things had been going better: Colonel Hamilton's artillery silenced the Boer guns on Pepworth, and drove most of the enemy off the summit; the Afrikaner positions were submitted to a positive hail of shrapnel shells, which were thudding down in batches of twenty and more; Boer dead and wounded were scattered over the hillside. Despite this success, Hamilton, denied the active and pre-arranged co-operation of Grimwood's brigade, felt disinclined to advance, and little more occurred in this sector of the battle area.

Further east, Grimwood's men came under determined Boer pressure. The Afrikaner commander Lukas Meyer, who had once established the petty republic of Vryheid, collapsed from nervous strain and left the field. His place was taken by his subordinate, and fellow founder of Vryheid, Louis Botha. Botha was intelligent and authoritative, a man of wide vision and considerable military competence – and destined to become one of the great Boer generals and the first Prime Minister of the Union of South Africa. Profiting from the arrival of reinforcements, Botha began to press hard against Grimwood's brigade – which was left virtually leaderless by its now unnerved commander.

Back in Ladysmith, General White grew despondent at the situation. He was threatened by a new Boer attack from the northeast, and morale had hardly been raised by the unexpected reappearance of Colonel Carleton's runaway artillery mules. The Boers' Long Tom on Pepworth Hill, moreover, had been steadily firing its massive 94-pound shells into Ladysmith, though it inflicted little damage; later a navy brigade arrived at Ladysmith, and promptly went out and silenced the Long Tom, but by 2 November the big 6-inch Creusot gun was again pounding away.

At any rate, White decided to recall his forces, and sent out a helio message to that effect. Hamilton's brigade made an orderly withdrawal, but Grimwood's men pulled back with a storm of Mauser bullets and shells whistling about their ears. Colonel Carleton's men at Tchrengula Mountain, however, received no order to withdraw, and were soon to be disgraced.

Carleton's position on Tchrengula quickly proved untenable, due to indifferent British leadership and expert Boer assaults. The Afrikaner commandos, led by the able Christiaan de Wet, wriggled stealthily towards the British defences shooting down any soldiers 51

that showed themselves or tried to withdraw. Soon the forward infantry units had been driven back. At this point one company of the Gloucesters, left stranded by their fellows, and believing that the main body of troops was marching back to Ladysmith, raised the white flag by tying a towel onto a sword.

British prisoners marching through Pretoria in the early days of the war.

This apparent surrender was soon reported to Colonel Carleton, who eventually ordered his bugler to sound the ceasefire. The wretched man struggled to produce the appropriate call, and at last gave out such a strangled blast that it was later rumoured that the Boers were responsible for it. More white flags were raised and the Boers waved their hats to acknowledge the ceasefire. A unit of the Irish Fusiliers saw things differently, however, and their enraged officers snapped their sword-blades across their knees in a dramatic gesture of protest. But it was of no avail, and more than eight hundred prisoners were taken by the Boers, who, according to

52

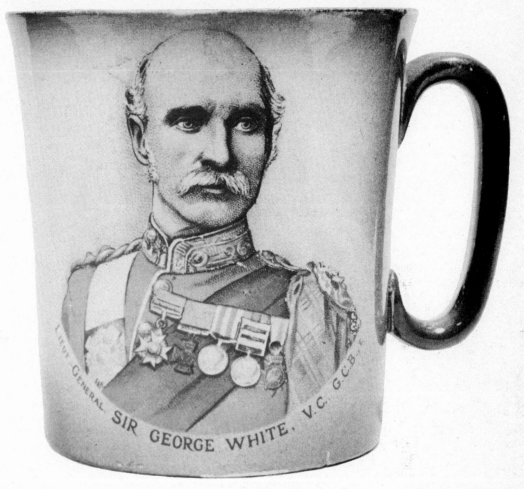

Dr Kay:

The defender of
Ladysmith, or a
different view of Sir
George White's mug!

told the dejected prisoners that they had heard them during the night
and by the time the day dawned they had two thousand men around the
hill.

They behaved very well to the wounded, riding some distance for
water and giving them blankets. One or two, however, were objection-
able, trying to loot medical stores and medical comforts, but on complaint being made to the Boer in command, he abused the looters and
sent them away calling them 'low Hollanders'. The prisoners had their
water-bottles, haversacks, glasses and anything of value taken from
them, and some were shoved about and treated roughly, but not the
wounded.

As some of the captured officers were talking to the triumphant
Boers, they caught sight of the British force of some ten thousand
men in full retreat for Ladysmith, great clouds of dust rising above   53

them. General Joubert deliberately held back from unleashing his horsemen upon them, subsequently explaining that 'When God holds out a finger, don't take the whole hand'.

For those besieged in Ladysmith there had been humiliation enough, and Dr Kay wrote on 31 October:

Yesterday, Mournful Monday, was the first day of the bombardment of the town after our defeat at Nicholson's Nek … and a mournful day for all of us. The Boers opened fire from Pepworth Hill at about 5.30 a.m. with their Long Tom, the first shot pitching near the station but doing no damage. The gun is a 6-inch Creuzot, one of the Pretoria Fort guns, a matchless advertisement for its French factory, for despite firing steadily all day it did little or no damage. We have christened it 'Puffing Billy'.

Nicholson's Nek turned out a disaster for us. Our men were so scattered because they had to cover such an enormous area of ground, the country so broken, and the mobility of the Boers turned to such good account, that we were forced to retreat. Some of our men being isolated and without support, retired at the double amid a great deal of confusion. The Boers followed and poured in very heavy fire with their mausers, their artillery using shrapnel and making excellent shooting, but luckily most of the shells burst too high. Had the Boers pressed home their advantage, there is little doubt that Ladysmith would have been taken that day.

Fortunately the Naval Brigade arrived at 10 a.m. They had managed to get through the Boer lines before they finally closed around us. I went to the railway station to meet them but they had no reception as all the troops and staff were busy engaged with the enemy.

Within half an hour the Brigade was on its way to the fight with their guns and maxims, and real good service they did, for their fourth shot either struck Puffing Billy or killed some of the men serving it, for the gun was silent for the rest of the day.

There was a dinner that night at the Royal Hotel for the officers of the Naval Brigade who were loudly cheered as their advent was both welcome and reassuring. There were many regular soldiers present, volunteers, war correspondents, civilians, and the usual hangers-on one meets in colonial towns. The situation was freely discussed and the general opinion was that the British had been outmanoeuvred and beaten, and that the Boers were very strong.

The General [White] and his staff were freely criticised; and there was almost a panic when later in the evening an officer came in and declared that the British losses were 30 killed, 97 wounded and 830 taken prisoner, and a mountain battery lost. Dismay was on every face, and all felt that bad times were in store.

With Ladysmith under siege, and British arms rebuffed in north Natal, the war was hardly going well for the Empire. In Britain, Arthur Balfour, First Lord of the Treasury and nephew of the Prime Minister, Lord Salisbury, told his sister Alice that he was surprised that at Ladysmith 'so large a garrison … amply supplied as I

54

believe they are with ammunition and food, can be in any danger ...
On the whole ... I am dissatisfied.'

Further afield than Ladysmith there were other causes for dissatisfaction. Mafeking and Kimberley needed to be relieved, yet there was no immediate prospect of this. Though the Boers had not been able to sweep into the potentially disloyal area of the northern Cape, they had shown resourcefulness and guile in their encounters with the British.

In Pretoria, Freda Schlosberg wrote in her journal:

2 November
A great multitude went to Pretoria station to witness the arrival of more British prisoners. The captured officers are said to be comfortably accommodated at the State Model School.

16 November
An armoured train is wrecked near Estcourt [in Natal] and an important man by the name of Winston Churchill is taken prisoner.

19 November
Sixty prisoners taken when the armoured train was wrecked near Estcourt, including this Mr Churchill, arrived at Pretoria at noon yesterday. Two officers and Mr Churchill were taken to the State Model School, and the rest of the prisoners to the Racecourse Prisoners Camp. Nobody was at the station to notice their arrival.

The general situation is splendid and hopeful for the Boers. Besieged Mafeking, Kimberley and Ladysmith are expected to surrender soon.

Meanwhile, in Mafeking, Soloman Plaatje, an erudite African interpreter at the local court, was writing elegantly in his diary:

Friday, 17th [November]
What a lovely morning after yesterday's rains. It is really evil to disturb a beautiful morning like this with the rattling of Mausers and whizzes and explosions of shells. 'Au Sanna' [the 94-pound Creusot siege gun] appears to have sharpened up, for her fire was very vigorous and quick since 3 o'clock. Mausers were also very brisk today. Goodness knows what these Boers are shooting: they kill on the average only one goat, sheep or fowl after spending five thousand rounds of Mauser ammunition – but very rarely a man.

Next day Plaatje wrote: 'We have just got definite information that the Troops [the Army Corps of fifty thousand men] landed at Cape Town on the 4th Instant and that they are given 6 days rest prior to proceeding north.' With Buller now safely disembarked, it seemed certain that a series of crushing blows would be delivered against the Boers. In the event, however, the British forces were on the brink of disaster.

Chapter 4

'Black Week' and its Prelude

At the end of November, British forces under Generals Gatacre and French moved against the threatened Boer invasion of the potentially rebellious northern Cape; in Natal, Buller established a huge base camp at Frere, twenty-five miles south of Ladysmith, where he mustered nearly twenty thousand amply equipped men; at the painfully gained Modder River station, some twenty-seven miles to the south of Kimberley, Lord Methuen was preparing to lead thirteen thousand men to the relief of the besieged diamond capital. During a single week in December, however, these three British offensives were each to suffer such serious rebuffs that the nation was finally shocked out of its lazy assumption that the war could be won quite easily.

The prelude to 'Black Week' was not altogether unsatisfactory for British arms, particularly in Lord Methuen's drive towards Kimberley – where Cecil Rhodes fretted like a caged lion. On 20 November, Methuen moved north from Orange River station, with a force of eight thousand men, which included the 9th Infantry Brigade and the Guards Brigade. He was in an aggressive mood, and not inclined to skirt the main obstacles that lay in his path, some groups of hills at Belmont and Graspan, the river at Modder River station, and a triangle of hills at Magersfontein. 'My good fellow,' Methuen said to a fellow officer who suggested a prudent detour round Belmont, 'I intend to put the fear of God into these people; and the only way is to fight them.'

Unfortunately, Methuen had become convinced by his reading of the Talana and Elandslaagte battles that direct attacks on Boer positions would be more fruitful than canny manoeuvres. He was, moreover, anxious to get to grips with the enemy, and to relieve Kimberley. He therefore proposed to push on along the railway line, repairing the sabotaged sections as he went.

Seventeen miles north of the Orange River the railway ran through Belmont station, where a group of hills (or kopjes) occupied by Afrikaners blocked the way. Methuen planned a night march and a dawn attack on the enemy positions on Table Mountain, Gun Hill and Mont Blanc. The 9th Infantry Brigade was to clear Table Mountain while the Guards drove the Boers from Gun Hill; then both brigades would sweep the enemy off Mont Blanc.

The plan went sadly awry. The Guards were late in taking up their positions, having been held up while cutting their way through wire fences; by the time they were ready it was nearly light, and the element of surprise had vanished. The Boers on the hills began

Opposite Joseph Chamberlain (Colonial Secretary 1895–1903) giving a confused John Bull a lesson in brink-manship 1899-style.

57

firing rapidly at their foes. The 1st Scots Guards and the 3rd Grenadiers nevertheless fixed bayonets and drove the Boers from Gun Hill. The Coldstreams meanwhile began attacking the wrong hills, to the south of Mont Blanc; though the 2nd Battalion was recalled, the 1st Battalion pressed on. The 9th Infantry Brigade were at the same time successfully storming Table Mountain.

Methuen let the disorganized conflict follow its own path, and was fortunate enough to see his infantry put the Boers to flight everywhere. After the battle he spoke to his men, praising them, and claiming that 'With troops like you no general can fear the result of his plans'.

The British troops rested at Belmont in the aftermath of this encounter. But on 24 November they were on the move again, marching northwards towards Graspan sidings on the railway line. Methuen's scouts told him that a mere five hundred Boers were on the Rooilaagte Hills near Graspan, but in fact by the time the British drew near there were 2,300 of them, composed of General Prinsloo's defeated men from Belmont and a commando unit led by the formidable Koos de la Rey. The Boers had three Krupp 75-mm guns and two pom-poms.

Methuen's guns began to bombard the enemy positions on the hills, but it was soon evident that this alone would not shift them. The General therefore sent the 9th Brigade and a naval detachment to capture the occupied eastern kopje, a hogsback running from north to south and dominating the surrounding hills. The sailors, marines, Northamptonshires, North Lancashires and the King's Own Yorkshire Light Infantry got to within a thousand yards of the enemy before the Boers opened fire. Enemy bullets did terrible damage among the closely packed ranks, and the officers, with their swords and glossy Sam Browne belts, were easily picked off. The advance continued to within two hundred yards of the kopje, when the survivors (about half the original force) lay down to fix bayonets and quench their thirst. Then they made their final charge, aided by men from the Northumberland Fusiliers from the north-east. The Boers broke and ran to their horses to escape. The British cavalry, exhausted by its reconnaissance work, was in no state to pursue them, and they made good their flight to the Modder River.

At the Modder River the Boers held a council of war. Prinsloo's Free Staters were dispirited by their recent defeats and some made off home. But de la Rey argued that the Boers would do better if they took up defensive positions as low down as possible, from which they could fire upon their enemies with a flat trajectory. Thus, lying close to the plain, they could sweep their front for over a mile in

Opposite Lieutenant-General Lord Methuen, who supervised the British disaster at Magersfontein during 'Black Week', 1899.

range. De la Rey managed to convince his fellow commanders, who now included Piet Cronje, that such a change in tactics would pay dividends; their smokeless powder would not give away the Boer positions, and they could expect to stop the British advance before the bayonet charge which they so much feared. The Afrikaners prepared their ground admirably, making use of the south banks of the Riet and Modder Rivers for shelter, and even placing white-washed posts and stones in front of them to ensure still more accurate fire.

On 28 November at 4 a.m. Lord Methuen's force began the march to Modder River station. The men were full of confidence, and a beautiful day was breaking over the veld. As they drew near to the banks of the Riet and the Modder, they little suspected the ambush that awaited them. Methuen himself was firmly convinced that a mere five hundred Boers blocked his path; he had, moreover, an inaccurate map which showed the River Riet running east to west, not south to north.

Methuen surveyed the river banks, and then said decisively to General Colville, 'They are not here.' Colville replied, 'They are sitting uncommonly tight if they are, sir.' As if in response, the Boers suddenly opened fire. Men fell on all sides, and if they had been allowed to approach any nearer the British would have been slaughtered wholesale. As it was, the Guards, on the right flank of the attack, were pinned down for hours under the scorching sun, unable to stir without inviting a hail of bullets.

On the left flank, the 9th Brigade had better luck, and some of them drove Prinsloo's Free Staters over the Modder towards Rosemead village. Lord Methuen, however, was wounded at 4.15 p.m. while observing this sector of the battle area and took no further part in the engagement. Prior to this he had moved freely along his front line and had consequently deprived his men of effective central control.

The 9th Brigade's success in crossing the Modder also included the eventual capture of Rosemead village. But elsewhere there was little progress. The British artillery poured over two thousand rounds into the Boers' positions, but hardly any real damage was inflicted. General Colville, who took over command from the wounded Methuen, toyed with the idea of a night attack on the Afrikaners, but eventually dropped the plan in view of the Guards' exhaustion after their gruelling day under the blazing sun.

Though the British hoped to exploit the uncertain situation the next day, they were doomed to disappointment for the Boers slipped
away under cover of darkness. Methuen had won the crossing of the

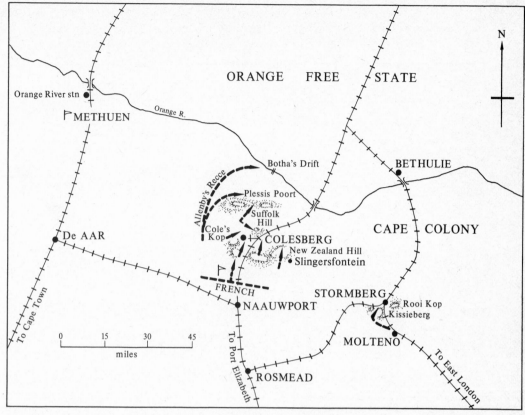

Modder, but at the cost of seventy dead and 413 wounded, or seven per cent of his force. He made the best of it by describing the battle as 'one of the hardest fights in the annals of the British Army'. Not all would have agreed with this description, and it was evident that more hard fighting would take place over the horizon where the Boers were digging trenches in front of the Magersfontein Hills.

The Battles of Stormberg, 9 December 1899, and Colesberg, 9 January 1900.

Before attempting to drive the Boers off the Magersfontein Hills, however, Lord Methuen gave his men (and himself) two weeks to recover from the battles of 23, 24 and 28 November. This rest, though perfectly sensible, gave the Afrikaners an invaluable period in which to prepare their defences, which consisted mainly of a line of camouflaged trenches at the foot of Magersfontein Hill.

While the Boers were digging in at Magersfontein, the first disaster of 'Black Week' occurred at the Battle of Stormberg on 10 December. Stormberg was fought to prevent Boer columns striking into the disloyal area of northern Cape Colony and encouraging disaffection and rebellion; the town was also on the junction of the railway lines between Port Elizabeth, East London and the Orange Free State.

61

Lieutenant-General
Gatacre, known as
'Backacher' to his
troops. Defeated at
Stormberg during
'Black Week',
December 1899.

On 9 December the gaunt, energetic General Gatacre (known to his troops as 'General Backacher') ordered three thousand men onto the train for Molteno, the nearest friendly station before Stormberg Junction. About 2,300 Boers, led by General Olivier, defended the pass that led to Stormberg. Gatacre was an over-enthusiastic exponent of the night march and the dawn attack, perhaps cherishing the illusion that he could thus bring off a coup as spectacular as Garnet Wolseley's brilliant victory at Tel-el-Kabir during the 1882 invasion of Egypt. On this occasion, however, things went badly wrong.

Although Gatacre's men were up at 4 a.m. on 9 December, due to bungled transport arrangements the entire force did not reach Molteno until 8.30 in the evening. It was not until 9.15 p.m. that men of the Irish Rifles and the Northumberland Fusiliers moved out of Molteno towards Stormberg Junction. Gatacre had decided that it was foolhardy to push on down the main pass, and instead planned to take the western end of a range of kopjes called the Kissieberg, from which he could dominate the route into Stormberg.

Unfortunately the one guide who knew the terrain well had been left behind, and Gatacre had to rely on guides who were soon lost and, worse still, refused to admit it. With bayonets fixed, the men stumbled on through the darkness; they had by now been without sleep for twenty-four hours, and were soon to fight a well rested enemy. As dawn broke the British force was actually behind the Kissieberg and moving in the wrong direction, whereas Gatacre believed that they were in front of it and about to advance into the railway pass!

Boer pickets on the eastern end of the Kissieberg suddenly saw the British beneath them. They gave the alarm and their comrades opened fire. Bereft of clear orders the British infantry hurled themselves heroically at the steep slopes of the hills; a few scrambled to the top of the range where they were dispersed by misdirected fire from their own artillery. In half an hour it was all over, and most of the battered and disorganized troops, fired on from two sides, were making an undignified retreat to Molteno. But six hundred men of the Northumberland Fusiliers had received no orders to withdraw and were left behind on the Kissieberg. Most of these were forced to surrender to the Afrikaners, which meant that, together with the ninety odd battle casualties, the British lost nearly seven hundred troops at Stormberg and the junction remained in enemy hands. So inexplicable did this reverse seem to the authorities in London that the news report, published on 11 December, claimed that Gatacre had been led into an ambush by treacherous guides. 63

64   Colonel Kekewich who quarrelled bitterly with Cecil Rhodes during the siege of Kimberley.

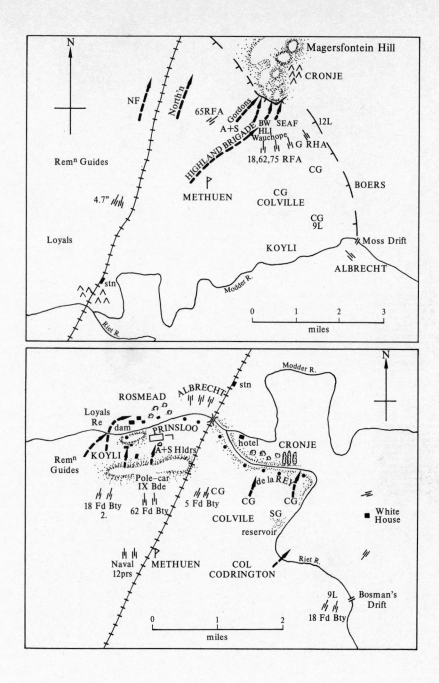

The Battles of Modder River, 28 November 1899 and Magersfontein (top), 11 December 1899.

On the same day that Gatacre's drive on Stormberg disintegrated, Lord Methuen was preparing to march on Kimberley, where an irate and jumpy Cecil Rhodes was at odds with the garrison commander, Colonel Kekewich, and inveighing against military men in general. Between Methuen and Kimberley lay the Magersfontein Hills, dominated on the right by Magersfontein Hill itself, upon whose slopes the Boers were entrenched. Methuen decided that the best way to carry Magersfontein Hill, and thus to open the way to Kimberley, was by an artillery bombardment followed by a dawn assault headed by the redoubtable Highland Brigade.

On Sunday 10 December Methuen's guns opened up on Magersfontein; the hill rocked under its one and a half hour's pounding, and it seemed certain to British observers that the Boer entrenchments must be shattered and the enemy dispersed. But ironically the vast bulk of Piet Cronje's force of 8,500 men were not on Magersfontein at all. They were concealed in a long line of narrow trenches running along the foot of Magersfontein and almost to the Modder River twelve miles away. The decision to forsake the traditional projection of the hills had been taken against Cronje's advice when the Free State's President Steyn had backed Koos de la Rey's plan to entrench an extended position on the plain at the base of Magersfontein.

The result of this tactical innovation was that the British walked straight into a devastating ambush. In the early hours of 11 December the Highland Brigade, composed of the Seaforths, the Gordons, the Argylls, the Black Watch and the Highland Light Infantry, moved off towards Magersfontein. Despite a violent storm overhead, and tacky going underfoot, the Highlanders had got to within half a mile of Magersfontein by 4 a.m. Their commander, Major-General Andy Wauchope, ordered them to extend their line prior to the assault. But as the four thousand men began to spread out, a murderous fusillade from the Boer trenches cut them to pieces. Within seconds hundreds were killed or wounded, and General Wauchope lay dead. Amazingly about a hundred Highlanders pressed on, broke through the trenches, and began climbing Magersfontein. But by an extraordinary coincidence, Piet Cronje and six of his adjutants, who were lost, wandered into their path and blazed away at them until reinforcements sealed the gap in the Boer entrenchments.

As the sun rose, the Afrikaners saw hundreds of the Highland Brigade lying face downwards on the sandy plain not daring to move. Despite a suicidal attempt by some men to rush the enemy's trenches, and a fitful skirl or two of the bagpipes, the majority of the

survivors sweated it out in the scorching heat until at about 1.30
p.m., by which time their morale had understandably crumbled,
they rose and escaped as best they could. When night fell hundreds
of wounded still lay unattended before the trenches.

The next day, 12 December, Methuen decided to order a general
withdrawal, after an armistice had allowed both sides to deal with
their dead and wounded. The Boers, as so often in this war, were
disinclined or unable to harry mercilessly the retreating British
troops. By 4 p.m. the shattered force was back at its camp on the
Modder River. Their losses were 210 killed and 738 wounded;
among the dead were Wauchope and the Marquis of Winchester; 67

British troops watching the progress of the ill-fated Battle of Colenso.

69

the leading companies of the Highland Brigade lost sixty per cent of their officers. The Afrikaners suffered comparatively trifling losses with eighty-seven killed and 188 wounded; Methuen's devastating bombardment of Magersfontein Hill had merely wounded three of the enemy.

Methuen must bear criticism for his generalship at Magersfontein. He set too much store on night marches and dawn attacks, which were risky and apt to exhaust the troops. He had no knowledge of the real Boer positions, and too few cavalry to reconnoitre properly. It is also arguable that he withdrew too soon, since his other brigades (including the Guards) were hardly thrown into the battle and might even have turned the Afrikaner flank.

As Methuen fell back onto the Modder river, General Buller was setting out with an army of eighteen thousand to dislodge eight thousand men under General Louis Botha from Colenso, where the railway and road to Ladysmith crossed the Tugela. The Boers were apprehensive at the coming battle, not merely because they were heavily outnumbered but also because of Buller's martial reputation. They need not have worried: Botha was a commander of supreme gifts, and Buller was about to reveal his inadequacies for all to see.

Sir George White, the beleaguered commander of Ladysmith, was expecting to co-ordinate with Buller's attack on Colenso by dispatching a sizeable field force against his Afrikaner besiegers. Unfortunately Buller failed to inform him of the date of his own attack, and the first that White knew of it was the rumble of guns across the Tugela. For two days Buller's artillery pounded Botha's positions. But the Boers gave nothing away: they did not budge, and their exact whereabouts remained a mystery to the British.

At dawn on 17 December Buller's men moved towards the Tugela. At the front Colonel Long forged ahead with twelve field pieces and six naval guns under his command. But within two hundred yards of the river the concealed Boers poured a withering fire into the field piece batteries. In under an hour hundreds of them had fallen, including the foolhardy Long, who shouted, though seriously wounded, 'Abandon be damned! We never abandon guns!' But the twelve field pieces could be defended no longer, and they were left useless and marooned on the banks of the Tugela.

Meanwhile, on the left flank, Major-General Hart muffed an attack with his Irish Brigade. A firm believer in strict discipline and close parade-ground order, Hart rashly led his unfortunate troops into the northern loop of the river where Botha's men were presented with a glorious target and the Irish Brigade was soon pinned down. British fortunes were no better on the right flank where de-

70

tachments of the Mounted Brigade made an unsuccessful attack on Hlangwhane, a hill that dominated Colenso to the west.

Buller, who had sat impassively watching these abortive assaults, munching some sandwiches, at last decided to withdraw. Dismayed that he had lost so many of his guns, he ordered a desperate rescue attempt which in fact succeeded in dragging two of the field pieces clear, though at the cost of several lives. Among those mortally wounded was Captain the Honourable F. H. S. Roberts, only son of Field-Marshal Lord Roberts of Kandahar. By a painful irony, Buller's indecisive tactics at Colenso not only contributed, indirectly, to Captain Roberts's death but also to the home government's decision to supersede him as Commander-in-Chief in South Africa with the bereaved Lord Roberts.

But Captain Roberts was not the only casualty at Colenso. The British lost 143 killed and 1,002 wounded. Botha's men lost a mere seven killed and twenty-two wounded, a result of their well entrenched positions and also of the smokeless powder contained in their cartridges which made their location difficult to assess.

The three disasters of 'Black Week' stunned the British public. There was a dichotomous response: on the one hand, patriots thumped the Imperial drum with renewed, even hysterical, vigour; on the other, a mounting volume of criticism was directed against the conduct of the war, and even against the justice of the British cause. *Punch* magazine tried to extract some wry humour from the enforced immobility of the British forces when it announced: 'Nigger News from Transvaal: De British hab got alongside o'Modder. But they habn't got no Farder.'

For Private Thomas Atkins, who was supposed to be 'wiping something off a slate' (the alleged indignities suffered by the Uitlanders plus the humiliation of Majuba Hill), there was little to laugh at. Earl de la Warr, on active service in South Africa, thought that the common soldier's lot in the campaign was a far from happy one:

Modder River, South Africa, December 25th. The battles in this campaign do not consist of a few hours' fighting, then a grand charge, resulting in the rout of the enemy, when men can see the effect of their work. No; this is very different. Think of it, a two-mile march under the fire of an invisible foe, then perhaps eight or ten hours' crouching behind any available cover – an ant hill or a scrubby bush – when the slightest movement on a man's part at once enables the hidden enemy to put him out of action, whereas he never has a chance of retaliating. Certainly this is fighting in circumstances which require extraordinarily good nerve and courage. And when the day is over 'Tommy' has not even the satisfaction of knowing what he has accomplished. When the day 71 comes which will give him an opportunity of getting at close quarters with the Boer, he will remember the long and weary hours he has spent facing the enemy's trenches.

Little of this chastened mood had yet percolated to those robust domestic patriots who were at this time revelling in the mawkish sentiment surrounding the story of the fourteen-year-old bugler, John Dunne, who had lost his bugle in the Tugela at the Battle of Colenso. Queen Victoria gave him a new bugle at Osborne, and the incident was preserved for a more cynical posterity in a popular verse:

> What shall we give, my little Bugelar,
> What for the bugle you lost at Tugelar?
> Give me another! that I may go
> To the front and return them blow for blow.

In Ladysmith, Dr Kay wrote, on 12 December: 'There was heavy firing Colenso way; it turns out Buller was repulsed and lost ten guns. Very serious for us, as no one knows when we shall be relieved. No one believes in our generals. If what the Russians said about our army in the Crimea was true, we are an army of lions led by asses.'

Aboard the SS *Induna* sailing from Lourenço Marques in Mozambique for Durban, the recently escaped Winston Churchill pondered over the implications of 'Black Week'. The defeats of Stormberg and Magersfontein had stiffened his resolve to escape, for he did not fancy the lengthy imprisonment implied by these Boer victories. So, aboard the *Induna*, Churchill composed a stirring cable for his paper the *Morning Post*, in which he argued that Britain could only negotiate with the Boers after achieving victory. He concluded:

> The individual Boer, mounted, in a suitable country, is worth four or five regular soldiers. The power of modern rifles is so tremendous that frontal attacks must often be repulsed. The extraordinary mobility of the enemy protects his flanks. The only way of treating them is either to get men equal in character and intelligence as riflemen, or, failing the individual, huge masses of troops ... We should show no hurry, but we should collect huge masses of troops. It would be much cheaper in the end to send more than is necessary. There is plenty of work here for a quarter of a million men, and South Africa is well worth the cost in blood and money. Are the gentlemen of England all fox-hunting? Why not an English Light Horse? For the sake of our manhood, our devoted Colonists, and our dead soldiers, we must persevere with the war.

In Britain, Arthur Balfour was one member of the government who had already formed a low opinion of Buller, telling his relation

The trenches from which the Boers decimated the British at the Battle of Magersfontein, December 1899.

Violet Cecil on 19 December 1899 that 'the case against him [Buller] could be made so strong that it is hard to justify retaining him in command even of a portion of our Army. He seems quite capable of forming a good plan, but quite incapable of sticking to it ... I think this is a most melancholy story and I can only account for it by the theory that for the last ten years Buller has allowed himself 73 to go downhill, and, for the moment at least, is not the man he once was.'

Queen Victoria, very old and almost blind, struggled to read the newspapers by candlelight during 'Black Week', and on one morning misread defeat for victory. Her high spirits at breakfast were promptly dampened by Princess Beatrice, her youngest child, who knew the truth. After a pause, the old Queen said, 'Now perhaps they will take my advice, and send our Lord Roberts and Lord Kitchener, as I urged them to do from the first.' When Balfour visited Windsor Castle at this time, Victoria was determined to uphold national morale, and told him plainly, 'Please understand that there is no one depressed in this house; we are not interested in the possibilities of defeat; they do not exist.'

The Queen was imbued with the desire to be of use to her people in these dark days. Though eighty years old, she undertook a strenuous round of military reviews and hospital visiting. She also sent off parcels of knitting to her 'dear brave soldiers'; when these gifts were appropriated instead by her dear brave officers, she had 100,000 tins of chocolates sent to the men. She was doubtless gratified to hear subsequently that one of these tins had stopped a Boer bullet!

The government, acting in concert with, though not in response to, the Queen's breakfast-time advice, decided in December 1899 to remove Buller from his command and replace him with Roberts and Kitchener. Lord Roberts, the new Commander-in-Chief in South Africa, was widely popular: he had won the VC during the Indian Mutiny, and further distinction during the Afghan War of 1879. A teetotaller, a believer in a form of national service, and of diminutive stature, Lord Roberts of Kandahar was known to the Victorian public as the 'Bobs' of Rudyard Kipling's poem:

> There's a little red-faced man,
>   Which is Bobs,
> Rides the tallest 'orse 'e can –
>   *Our* Bobs.
> If it bucks or kicks or rears,
> 'E can sit for twenty years
> With a smile round both 'is ears –
>   Can't yer, Bobs?

Kitchener of Khartoum, the victor of Omdurman, reserved, complicated and ruthless, went as Roberts's second-in-command. Roberts was enthusiastic at having Kitchener to serve under him. They were certainly an impressive team, and Roberts dismissed doubts as to his own physical vigour and age (he was sixty-seven) with the words 'for years I have led a most active and abstemious life, waiting for this day'. Roberts's appointment was rendered almost agonizingly poignant by the heroic death of his only son at Colenso.

But the man whose blunders had been chiefly responsible for the Colenso defeat, Sir Redvers Buller, was still in command in South Africa, waiting for Roberts's arrival. Before he could be superseded, Buller (nicknamed 'Sir Reverse' and the 'Ferryman of the Tugela') led his men in another drive to relieve Ladysmith.

Chapter 5

The Battles of Spion Kop and Vaal Krantz

Though Buller knew that he would soon be released from the burden of the overall command of British forces in South Africa, he was still commander in north Natal, and in fact he made three further attempts to relieve Ladysmith. Two of these, resulting in the Battles of Spion Kop and Vaal Krantz, were to be added to the list of the unfortunate Buller's blunders.

The Battle of Spion Kop was fought on 24 January 1900. It was hardly the New Year's gift that the Empire wanted at the opening of the century that was to witness its eventual decline and disintegration. Indeed it ranks as possibly the sharpest defeat of the war, and made such an impact on public opinion at home that football grounds from Liverpool to Northampton named their high terraced ends 'the Kop' or 'Spion Kop'.

Buller's preparations for the battle were characteristically thorough. He was not the man to fight on an empty stomach, and he ensured that his troops should not do likewise. Nor did he believe in the heroic exertions of 'thin red lines' of ill equipped men: he built up substantial forces with which to campaign, and guaranteed them ample supplies and creature comforts.

By the beginning of January, Buller had thirty thousand men under his command in north Natal, with the addition of a new division under General Sir Charles Warren. On 16 January 1900 he set off with 24,000 infantry, 2,500 mounted troops, eight field batteries and ten naval guns, planning to cross the Tugela at Trichardt's Drift and 'gain the open plain north of Spion Kop'. To do this he proposed to send Warren's division on a sweeping left flanking movement round the Rangeworthy Hills then on eastwards to the town of Dewdrop where it would link up with General Lyttelton's brigade forging up from the south over Potgieter's Drift. The Boer's hill entrenchments would thus have been turned, and the combined columns could press on to Ladysmith fifteen miles away.

At first the advance went well. The Tugela was efficiently bridged and the troops and their bountiful supplies taken across in excellent order. Lord Dundonald's cavalry moved in a great leftwards arc towards Acton Homes on the road to Ladysmith. To their rear, General Warren found the route too difficult for his wagons; he therefore halted at Fairview at the foot of the Rangeworthy Hills. Calling back Dundonald's cavalry, he now proposed to dislodge the Boers by a direct attack on the hills. Surveying the terrain he decided to occupy the highest peak on the ridge – Spion Kop. From this

Opposite Dazed British troops picking up the pieces after their disastrous defeat at Spion Kop.

77

vantage point he could then enfilade the Afrikaner trenches and dominate the Fairview-Rosalie road to Ladysmith.

After obtaining grudging approval from Buller for his assault on Spion Kop, General Warren divided his force into a Left Attack and a Right Attack. The latter group, under Major-General Coke, was chosen to seize Spion Kop, though Lieutenant-Colonel Thorneycroft, who had sketched out the landmarks on the route up the mountain, actually acted as guide. The assault column set off before midnight, and grappled in the mist with the steep, rock-strewn slope of Spion Kop, fearing detection at any moment. But in fact the men managed to attain the summit before a Boer picket challenged them, and were able to dislodge the seventy or so Afrikaners with a brisk bayonet charge. At 4 a.m. on 24 January Spion Kop was in British hands.

For three hours, while the mist hung over the summit, the troops dug themselves in. But the hard ground prevented the construction of anything more than a dangerously shallow entrenchment with a parapet. Then, at about 7 a.m., the mist began to lift, revealing the true situation. The British had won only part of the summit. Worse still, their entrenchments were pitifully exposed to enemy fire from all directions; field guns, pom-poms and rifles could be directed at the British positions. Within an hour the Lancashire Fusiliers, the Scottish Rifles and Thorneycroft's mounted infantry were being systematically shot to pieces. The Lancashire Fusiliers were caught in a terrible enfilade fire from the Twin Peaks to the east, and soon their shallow trench was piled high with bodies. Soon the surviving Lancashires were waving white handkerchiefs, or trying to slip off down the hill. The redoubtable Thorneycroft, reinforced by men of the Middlesex Regiment and the Imperial Light Infantry, managed, however, to retrieve the situation on the summit and, with further assistance from the Scottish Rifles, held the hill-top for the rest of the day.

Bad though the British position on Spion Kop had proved to be, it was made worse by Buller's generalship. There was great confusion as to who was in command at the summit: General Woodgate, the brigade commander, was severely wounded, and Buller at last told General Warren to put Thorneycroft in charge; but Major-General Coke, the officer commanding the Right Attack, and Lieutenant-Colonel Hill of the Middlesex Regiment, were mysteriously not informed of this crucial decision. More serious still was Buller's reaction to the success of General Lyttelton's brigade, which had crossed the Tugela at Potgieter's Drift and then stormed the Twin Peaks, east of Spion Kop and the source of some

Opposite David Lloyd George, up-and-coming Liberal MP, and a leading 'pro-Boer'.

79

The Tugela Campaign: the sites of the Battles at Rietfontein, Lombard's Kop (Ladysmith), Nicholson's Nek, Wagon Hill, Colenso, Spion Kop, Vaal Krantz and Pieter's Hill.

of the most destructive enfilading fire. Lyttelton's triumph on the Twin Peaks was not in accordance with Buller's overall plan, and at sunset the troop was recalled. A real chance of averting defeat was thus cast away.

Night fell with Thorneycroft still holding on to the summit. But when the young war correspondent Winston Churchill managed to reach Thorneycroft in the darkness with messages from Warren, he found that the summit commander had decided to withdraw. Churchill was shocked at the sight of the exhausted, wounded and dead troops on Spion Kop, and appreciated Thorneycroft's conviction that he had been sacrificed to the incompetence of his superiors who had allowed thousands of fresh troops to stand idly by while he and his men had struggled for survival.

But even as Thorneycroft's men were staggering down from the summit, the Boers were similarly drifting away from Spion Kop. An earlier assault on the British position by nearly nine hundred of the enemy had been beaten back; and Lyttelton's temporary occupation of the Twin Peaks was an ominous challenge. At about 2 a.m., however, the tireless efforts of Louis Botha halted the Boer dispersal. As the Afrikaners reluctantly returned to the foot of Spion Kop some of them saw in the breaking dawn two men on the summit waving their hats in triumph; they had scaled the hill and found it deserted.

The British had withdrawn first, thus handing victory to their opponents. Buller insisted on a complete retreat across the Tugela, which he supervised with his characteristic care. But he had lost 1,750 men killed, wounded and captured on Spion Kop, while the Boers had lost a mere three hundred. Moreover, Ladysmith had not been relieved.

Spion Kop was a British defeat partly because both Buller and Warren stuck to plans which Dundonald's cavalry dash towards Acton Homes and Lyttelton's occupation of the Twin Peaks ought to have been allowed to amend: communications between the senior officers involved had been appalling. Nor did the British, once Thorneycroft had accepted defeat, have anyone of the calibre of Botha to rally their men for one last effort.

The news of this 'sickening fiasco', as Joseph Chamberlain called it, struck Britain like a thunderbolt. Accusations of muddle and incompetence multiplied. Lloyd George and the 'pro-Boers' redoubled their criticisms of the war, and the great powers of Europe took further delight in British discomfiture.

Even before the disaster of Spion Kop, the poor showing of British arms had provoked recrimination and fostered discontent.

Black women and
children amidst a white
man's war.

Arthur Bigge, Queen Victoria's Principal Private Secretary, had
written to the influential Balfour on 2 January 1900:

> No-one has ever laid down what is expected of our army – until this is
> done we shall never have a satisfactory organized force. If only someone
> in authority could have realized that we might be called upon to conduct
> a campaign against 45,000 Boers fully armed and equipped, and we had
> organized accordingly – not forgetting India, our other colonies and
> Home Defence – we might have been better prepared. However I see
> that you think everything has now been supplied to the Generals but
> brains! In these I imagine the Primate is arranging a special day of
> intercession!

Balfour himself was privately gloomy at the prospects, before
knowing the full details of Spion Kop, telling his brother-in-law
Henry Sidgwick on 24 January, 'I not only think blunders have been
committed, but I think they have been of the most serious kind,
imperilling the whole progress of the war. But I do not think those
blunders are due to War Office maladministration ... The chief

blunders have been made, in my private opinion, by our Generals in the field.'

In Ladysmith, Dr Kay wrote on 27 January:

Headquarters received very bad news from Buller yesterday but wouldn't let it out. Today's *Orders* state that last Wednesday [24 January], after shelling the Boers for a whole week, General Warren took the Boer position at Spion Kop, fourteen miles from here, but the Boers made a night attack and re-took it, and of course there's the usual remark, 'The Boer losses were very heavy.' We all expected bad news and now we have it with a vengeance. Everyone is very down and depressed. 'Measurable distance' now means a dozen of Buller's promises.

After the Battle of Spion Kop there was a two-week lull in the campaign in north Natal. Many Boers retired to their laagers around Ladysmith, or went home to rest and see their families. Among their high command there was a good deal of skirmishing as to who should take charge of the forces besieging Ladysmith: President Kruger did not want Prinsloo, the nominee of President Steyn of the Orange Free State; Joubert did not want the position, and eventually it was given to Louis Botha.

On the British side, Buller made plans for a third offensive to clear the path to Ladysmith. The plans were complicated, though well considered. Unfortunately their execution was marred by Buller's vacillation and lack of confidence.

On 5 February his troops moved off to oust the enemy from a group of hills some six miles to the east of Spion Kop; the Tugela would have to be crossed, and then an assault mounted on Vaal Krantz, Green Hill and Doorn Kop which guarded the eastern route to Ladysmith. Buller proposed to bluff the Boers by a diversionary attack to the west of Vaal Krantz via a specially constructed pontoon bridge; the real attack was to go in further east, again over a pontoon bridge.

The opening stages of the operation were reasonably successful. The diversionary advance westwards began well, but unfortunately more field batteries than planned went over the western pontoon; some of these batteries were needed for the genuine eastern push, so three vital hours were lost while the missing batteries were retrieved. The Royal Engineers worked heroically at the pontoon bridges, completing the eastern one in fifty minutes though under persistent rifle and Maxim gun fire. The artillery had meanwhile subjected the Boer positions to a heavy bombardment.

All was now set for a successful climax to the operation. The Durham Light Infantry and the Rifle Brigade crossed the eastern 83

Paul Kruger, President of the Transvaal and arch-opponent of British supremacy. He died
in exile in Switzerland two years after the war ended.

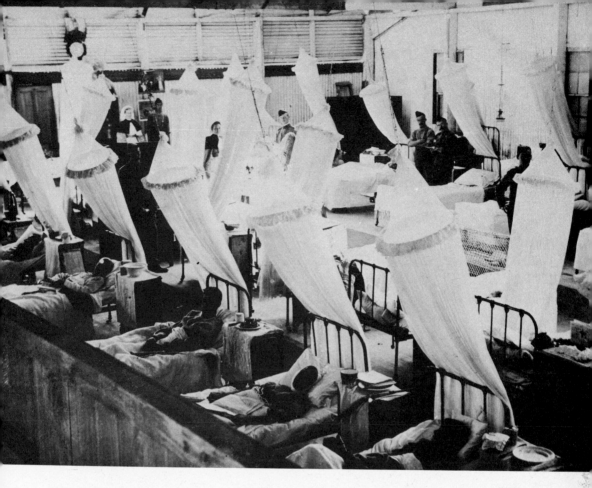

pontoon bridge, and though coming under heavy fire made straight for their objectives; the Durhams moved rapidly through mealie fields towards the foot of Vaal Krantz, while the Rifle Brigade cleared the enemy from their position at Munger's Farm.

At this point, Buller's nerve gave way. Fire from Green Hill and Doorn Kop to the west was disconcertingly heavy. Accordingly he decided to break off the attack and forbade the 60th Foot and the Scottish Rifles to go to the support of General Lyttelton and the troops approaching Vaal Krantz. The enraged and astounded Lyttelton pointed out that his men were already committed to the attack, and reluctantly Buller allowed the 60th and the Scottish Rifles to cross the pontoon bridge. He still kept back the forces that were meant to take Green Hill, however, as well as the cavalry. Lyttelton's infantry pressed on, and eventually took the southern-most hill of the Vaal Krantz ridge – which was all that Buller authorized them to do. Despite enfilading fire, the men managed to shelter behind loose rocks and thus avoided heavy casualties. Night fell with the main attack aborted by Buller's indecision.

A far cry from Florence Nightingale! Well-cared-for British wounded in hospital in East London, Cape Colony. Note the mosquito nets.

85

Bottle party on the veld.
British troops take a
break.

In his despair, Buller sent a telegram to his newly arrived Commander-in-Chief Lord Roberts, who was about to strike across the
Modder River and relieve Kimberley. Roberts had not wanted
Buller to launch his third attack across the Tugela, since he
believed that his own advance through the Free State would ease
the pressure in north Natal. But now that Buller had committed
himself to a fresh offensive, he saw no convincing reason why the
operation should be called off. Thus, in reply to Buller's query as to
whether to persevere, Roberts stated that in his opinion the attack
should go forward, and that the troops' morale should be boosted
by the message that if they relieved Ladysmith they would also
strike a great blow for the honour of the Empire.

Even in the face of Roberts's advice, Buller dithered in a crisis of self-confidence. But on 8 February he made up his mind to withdraw – something, at least, that he always did with considerable finesse and good sense. He fell back, through Springfield, to Chieveley, the base from which he had started out a month before. There he began to plan yet another offensive, but was unable to achieve his long awaited breakthrough until 27 February.

Though he managed to keep his troops' morale reasonably high through good feeding and care, Buller prompted the war correspondent J. B. Atkins to write after the Battle of Vaal Krantz: 'The fault of this and all other battles, was the cumbrous nature of our transport. How should it be otherwise than that jam and pickles should be at a disadvantage against biltong?' But in Ladysmith there was little enough jam and pickles; indeed food supplies were almost exhausted, and 'waiting for Buller' had become a macabre and hungry game. The privations of Ladysmith were soon to be ended, however, as were those of Kimberley. The relief of Mafeking would take a little longer.

Chapter 6

The Besieged Towns: Ladysmith, Kimberley and Mafeking

The siege of Ladysmith lasted from October 1899 to the end of February 1900 – 118 days in all. The Boers encircled the town within a six-mile radius, mostly from hill positions like Pepworth, Gun Hill, Long Hill, Lombard's Kop, Middle Hill, Umbulwana, Rifleman's Ridge, Lancer's Hill, Telegraph Ridge and Tchrengula. The British manned a smaller defensive ring within the Boer circle, taking up positions on Observation Hill, Tunnel Hill, Rifleman's Post and Bester's Ridge. General White placed his headquarters upon Convent Hill, from which central site he could oversee the town's defences.

Boer tactics were quite straightforward. They planned to starve and bombard Ladysmith into surrender, while keeping the inept Buller at bay along the Tugela. The Afrikaner forces made only one major attempt to break through the British defensive circle by an assault on Bester's Ridge on 6 January 1900.

For the soldiers (some ten thousand of them) and the civilians of Ladysmith, the siege required reserves of patience rather than deeds of heroic self-sacrifice. Eyewitness accounts of the siege are particularly revealing and interesting. For example, Colonel R. W. Mapleton was the Principal Medical Officer in charge of the Ladysmith hospital, and was later allowed by the Boers to set up a neutral camp at Intombi (some four miles south-east of the town) where the wounded and non-combatants could take refuge. He wrote, in a number of letters:

> We are besieged by a large force of Boers, and although we have ten thousand men here we can't get out and so are waiting until we are relieved. We had about three very hot days in Ladysmith as the Boers shelled the town and the shells were screaming and bursting all over the place and considering the number of shells very few people were hit though there were many narrow escapes. I had no particular near-shave myself but one lump of shell about six by four inches fell pretty close to me and nearer to where I had passed. Such a lot of shells fell into and about the hospital that on the representation of Sir George White to Joubert, all the hospitals moved out to a bit of neutral ground four miles from the town and here we are now. We are close to the enemy position and can see them with the naked eye. I think we are all glad to get out of here for the shell-fire was too hot to be pleasant and someone must have been hit if we had stayed where we were.
>
> I have seen some of the Boers for as I am in charge of the hospital out here, I have several times met the Boers under a flag of truce to discuss sundry matters. Those I have seen have all been very pleasant fellows indeed and very friendly. They have behaved extremely well to our wounded prisoners, attending to them and giving them everything they had themselves. All our wounded speak highly of the kindness they have received at their hands ...

Opposite Sterling stuff! £1 siege note issued at Mafeking in March 1900.

The bullet the Boers use is an extraordinary missile: it is about one
and a quarter inches long and as thin as a lead pencil. It incapacitates a
man but it does not kill him like the old Martini and other bullets. I have
seen men shot through the brain, matter oozing out of the hole in the
skull and yet the man recovered very shortly too. Men shot through the
lungs have very little trouble from the wounds. If it catches a hard bone
it at times smashes it, but generally drills a hole right through it. The
shell wounds are of course ghastly to a degree ...

The shops are all shut in Ladysmith, and some of the civil population
have been cleared out into this camp which is a very big one ... We get
lots to eat though I dare say you would turn up your snout at it, for the
quality though all right for camp is not what one would select for choice,
still besieged people have to be thankful for what they can get. The water
is like pea soup but we boil it and filter it.

A good deal of big gun firing goes on all day, and now and again the
Boers let off all their guns into the town at midnight – no one knows why.
They have knocked down a lot of houses in Ladysmith but have done
comparatively little damage. Two of our officers were sitting side by side
having lunch at the hotel; a shell burst just outside the house, and a big
lump of it came through the window and actually went between them
as they sat, and hurt no one. Pretty close shave that! One shell came into
our camp, but did not burst, but rolled through the camp and through
a tent and hurt no one. Many shells have burst close to people and not
hurt them. One burst in a room in which were thirteen people, and no
one was hurt. Of course there is a reverse side of the picture.

I get about fifty-five sick a day into this hospital, and I am now in
charge of no less than 1,270 sick and wounded, including sixty-five
officers. I have a very insufficient staff of both officers and men to do the
enormous amount of work: about 500 cases of enteric fever, 180 of
dysentery and 150 wounded.

Dr Alec Kay's letters are also an excellent record of the conditions in Ladysmith. Dr Kay became increasingly disillusioned with the game of 'waiting for Buller', and wrote savagely of Britain's 'phantom army'. His morale was doubtless boosted by being allowed a brief leave on Christmas Day 1899, when he left Intombi Camp for Ladysmith. He saw a room at the back of the Standard Bank at Ladysmith, which had been decorated 'very nicely and there were four Christmas trees labelled, "Canada", "Australia", "Britain" and "South Africa". At 7 p.m. all the children in Ladysmith were to be there – plenty of cakes, lemonade and other things for them. I trust they enjoyed themselves.'

Dr Kay then walked, with some friends, to the naval camp, where he recorded in a letter to his wife, Alice:

> From there we walked slowly up to the naval camp. The Boers had not fired a shot all day. Just as we got there their guns began plugging away and put in shell after shell as hard as they could, which riled everyone, thinking Christmas Day should be 'Peace on earth and goodwill towards all men'. I am very glad that they did so, as it shows what swines they are. And yet that very morning the gun on Bulwana fired two shots, the shells pitching in the town without exploding. When dug up, they were found to be stuffed with rough plum pudding and outside on the shell was painted 'A Merry Christmas'. Which forced many to say or think, 'There is some humour and some good in the Boers after all.' One of these shells was bought by a curio hunter for £15. The subsequent shelling dispelled these favourable thoughts about them and made some of us very savage.
>
> When we got to the mess tent I had a long whisky and soda – the first one for ages; I shall never forget that drink, it was over too soon.
>
> At about seven o'clock Captain Lampton came in and we prepared for dinner. Am glad sailors are superstitious, as thirteen were going to sit down, so they sent for a petty officer who came in to make it fourteen.
>
> We had excellent soup, turkey, sucking pig and plum pudding – a real good one both for quality and size. Sherry, champagne-and-stout (black velvet) and whisky and soda ad lib. A toast to Her Most Gracious Majesty the Queen, which we most enthusiastically drank. Then someone, riled by the Boer shelling that day, proposed, 'To Hell with the Boers!' which we drank with enthusiasm and laughter, considering the surroundings. It was the most enjoyable and successful dinner it was possible to have.
>
> After dinner a lot of the 19th Hussars came in, and officers of other regiments, and a lively time it was.
>
> I thoroughly enjoyed myself, and was very sorry to return at 5.15 a.m. to Intombi Camp.

But after the Christmas festivities, which were evidently reasonably lavish, the grim realities of the siege were re-asserted. The 'music of the guns' accompanied the worsening of conditions within Ladysmith and its environs:

The sight of our men washing so infuriated the Boers that they immediately opened fire.

The Boers ruining the ablutions of the sturdy defenders of Ladysmith – from a contemporary sketch.

27 December

There was a false alarm that the Boers were attacking the town, but our men did not fire. We could see the flashes of the rifles and a line of fire to the right.

Every now and then we are cheered up with the news 'Buller is certain to be here on such and such a day', but it is one disappointment after another.

They say 'Everything comes to he who waits' but oh, it is a very weary waiting, especially on an empty stomach.

I have just been told that there's a reliable runner leaving at any minute. So in haste and with lots of love to you all,

Your ever loving,
Alec

On 21 February, Dr Kay gave an account of the soaring prices of food and luxuries in the besieged town:

21 February

The prices of luxuries are astounding. I myself paid £5 for four tins of milk, £3 for a bottle of port, £7 for a bottle of whisky, and I am sure that if £20 had been offered no one who had it would have parted with it. I was ill at the time, and I believe that it meant life to me. A tin of condensed milk was always cheap at £1 and when I bought four tins I could easily have made a substantial profit had I waited to sell. Here is a list of prices published by Joe Dyson, an auctioneer in Ladysmith:

	£	s.	d.
14 lb. Oatmeal	2	19	6
Condensed milk, per tin		10	0
1 lb. beef fat		11	0
1 tin coffee		17	0
2 lb. tin of tongue	1	6	0
1 sucking pig	1	17	0
Eggs, per dozen	2	8	0
Fowls, each		18	6
4 small cucumbers		15	6
Green mealies, each		3	8
1 small plate of grapes	1	5	0
1 small plate of apples		12	6
1 plate of tomatoes		18	0
1 vegetable marrow	1	8	0
1 plate of potatoes		19	0
3 small bunches of carrots		9	0
1 glass jar jelly		18	0
1 lb. bottle of jam	1	11	0
1 lb. tin of marmalade	1	10	0
1 doz. boxes matches		13	6
1 packet of cigarettes	1	5	0
50 cigars	9	5	0
½ lb. cake 'Fair Maid' tobacco	2	5	0
¼ lb. „ „ „ „	3	5	0
1 lb. Sailors tobacco	2	3	0
¾ lb. tin 'Capstan' Navy tobacco	3	0	0

The Boer guns have been pounding us incessantly. Their shooting is remarkably good, superior to ours. Their Long Toms are six-inch Creuzots and are heavier than our 4·7 naval guns which however have greater range and greater penetration. The ordinary Boer field guns are far superior to ours – greater range and higher velocity; but our gunners say they are much heavier, which naturally means they are less mobile and require more horses, but I am not sure they are right for I have myself seen the Boer pieces going across country with only six horses and at a good gallop – as fast as our artillery go with their guns and they are only twelve-pounders. Many of their gunners are French or German.

We frequently hold open-air concerts at Intombi. If the music is not first-class and the songs are not drawing-room, we none the less appreciate them.

The defenders of Ladysmith had other discomforts. The heat, during the South African summer, was often intense, and on 17 February 1900 Dr Kay wrote, 'Heat lately has been awful, temperature in my tent 116 degrees [farenheit] with an accurate thermometer.' There

93

were scorpions and tarantulas; the bread was 'as hard as stones and with no more nutrition. It often produces violent pains and diarrhoea ... Matches are scarce and candles are unobtainable ... The amount of theft in Ladysmith and at Intombi is astounding.'

Sir George White was not completely supine during these long weeks. There were some ill-fated attempts to co-operate with Buller's sporadic relief operations, and an ineffective cavalry sortie took place. Two attacks were made on Boer gun positions during December 1899: the first attack destroyed a 4·7-inch howitzer and the Long Tom on Gun Hill; the second succeeded in knocking out another 4·7 howitzer on Surprise Hill. These forays were expensive, however: seventy-five British soldiers were killed or wounded, and the Long Tom was repaired at Pretoria in three weeks and dispatched to the siege of Kimberley.

On 6 January 1900 the Boers made their one full-scale attempt to break through the British defences when they attacked Bester's Ridge (or the Platrand); there were three hills comprising this ridge – Wagon Point to the west, Wagon Hill in the centre, and Caesar's Camp to the east. The Afrikaners planned to assault the ridge with two thousand men, while three thousand more would give support if necessary, or make a diversionary attack against Observation Hill to the north of Ladysmith. The Transvaal commandos were to be led by the republic's Vice-President, Schalk Burger, and the Free Staters by General de Villiers; the overall command was given to Piet Joubert, accompanied by his sharp-eyed wife who had proved herself an able tactician twenty years earlier at Majuba Hill.

On the British side, the inspiring and doughty Ian Hamilton was in command of the one thousand men defending Bester's Ridge. Though Caesar's Camp was well fortified, Wagon Hill had only two fortified posts. The Manchester Regiment was stationed at Caesar's Camp, while the Imperial Light Horse, dismounted, and the 60th held Wagon Hill and Wagon Point; the Gordon Highlanders provided reinforcements, as did other units of dismounted cavalry.

The men defending Wagon Hill and Wagon Point were the first to be aware of the Boer approach. This was partly fortuitous, since units of infantry were guarding sappers who were preparing gun pits for two naval guns.

At 2.45 a.m. the advancing columns of Afrikaners were challenged by British troops, and the two sides began to blaze away in the darkness. In the confusion, the Gordons mistook the slouch-hatted
Imperial Light Horse for the enemy and were on the point of

shooting them down. Hand-to-hand fighting took place, while the British officers tried to organize their lines of defence. Caesar's Camp was apparently secure, so Hamilton, awoken by the firing, sent a message calling for reinforcements to Sir George White, and then went off to Wagon Hill.

At Wagon Hill, the British were being hard pressed by units of Free Staters. As day broke, neither side could dislodge the other from their positions. Not long after midday, however, the Boers made a determined attempt to oust the British from the 4·7-inch gun emplacement on Wagon Point; happily, from their point of view, they caught a considerable number of troops literally napping. Many of the British troops stumbled, panic-stricken, down the hill, while Hamilton and some of his officers and NCOs tried desperately to check the disorderly rout. Hamilton was ably supported by Lieutenant Digby Jones of the Royal Engineers and Trooper Albrecht of the cavalry; together they led a counter-charge which scattered the Boers and sent them scurrying from the summit. Both Digby Jones and Albrecht were killed in this action, and were posthumously awarded the Victoria Cross.

More reinforcements came up, mostly composed of dismounted cavalrymen. But the hills were still tenanted by Boers. At 5.30 p.m. the Manchesters managed to drive the enemy from the edge of

An assortment of the military hardware fired into Ladysmith during the siege 1899–1900.

Caesar's Camp. Sir George White, however, wanted Wagon Hill cleared by nightfall too. Hamilton passed on this order to the Devonshires, confident that they would carry out their mission. The Devonshires promptly made an heroic bayonet charge at the enemy, cheering as they went, and falling like ninepins; other units joined them. Half an hour later darkness fell, and the worsted Boers slipped away, a good many of them drowning in the flooded Fouries Spruit.

The attack on Caesar's Camp and Wagon Hill had failed. There were four hundred British casualties, some two hundred Afrikaner losses. Both sides had displayed remarkable bravery as well as cowardice. White made haste to tell Buller that he could no longer co-operate in any further attempts to relieve Ladysmith. At home, the sixteen-hour struggle had raised fears that Ladysmith would fall, and the situation was viewed gloomily. Even by 7 January, when it was evident that the Boers had been repulsed, British opinion remained jittery, and there were some who now reconciled themselves to the inevitable surrender of the besieged town.

The siege of Kimberley lasted from 15 October 1899 to 16 February 1900. At Kimberley, four thousand Boers hemmed in the five hundred British troops and some fifty thousand civilians. There were about thirteen thousand Europeans, seven thousand coloureds (of mixed blood) and thirty thousand Africans. In one sense, Kimberley belonged to Cecil Rhodes and de Beers, his great diamond-mining company. Appropriately enough, Rhodes was in Kimberley, and de Beers supplied 450 rifles to the defenders, as well as being able to manufacture ammunition in its workshops. The commanding officer was Colonel Kekewich; apart from his five hundred regulars, 3,500 civilians were eventually enrolled in the Town Guard.

Compared with the sieges of Ladysmith and Mafeking, Kimberley's ordeal lacked some of the military melodrama of Buller's campaign in north Natal, or the lengthy timespan of Mafeking's encirclement. The garrison was not idle, however, and made a number of sorties against the enemy. One of the most important of these expeditions took place the day before Lord Methuen fought the Battle of Modder River on 28 November. Three columns left Kimberley, planning to attack the Boers on Carter's Ridge five miles west of the town. Though the British force did tolerably well, they failed to take Carter's Ridge, and withdrew at nightfall having sustained fifty-six casualties; nor were they able to break through and give first-hand assistance to Lord Methuen. The foray did, however, succeed in engaging part of the besieging force, just as the defence of Kimberley itself effectively pinned down four thousand of the enemy who might otherwise have raised rebellion in northern Cape Colony.

Kimberley was never in real danger of being taken by the Boers. There were no dominating, surrounding kopjes from which the Boers could bombard the town, though they did manage to situate some siege guns on the few low ridges nearby. Kimberley's mining economy also aided the defenders in a variety of ways: heaps of mining debris, sixty to seventy feet high, were used as perimeter strongpoints; an observation tower was built on top of a mine shaft's hauling gear, and, connected by telephone to the perimeter strongpoints, ensured that any enemy movements in the surrounding countryside would be quickly spotted; de Beers lent powerful searchlights with which to survey the surroundings at night.

Nor did Kimberley suffer the acute food shortages of Ladysmith and Mafeking, though towards the end of the siege many civilians seem to have endured considerable hardship. The African element in the population were particularly unfortunate: a large number of their babies and infants died from lack of milk, and scurvy also affected many African adults. It was fortunate that de Beers had a large stock of food and fuel. Colonel Kekewich also took the sensible step of issuing a proclamation fixing the price of basic commodities at the pre-siege figure. From time to time, moreover, bands of Africans raided Boer herds, and thus supplemented the town's food supply.

The main drama at Kimberley, in fact, involved the clash between Cecil Rhodes and Colonel Kekewich. Rhodes, restless, preoccupied and barely two years away from death, was not content to wait passively for Methuen, or even for Roberts and French; he was, moreover, bitterly critical of Kekewich's handling of the town's defences. As early as 16 October, Rhodes sent a message to Milner in Cape Town, using the heliograph link from Kimberley to the next telegraph station, and saying: 'Strain everything. Send immediate relief to Kimberley. I cannot understand the delay.' The next day Rhodes set the mirrors flashing again, while local wags guessed he must be selling or buying shares; this time he sent a message, via Lord Rothschild in London, to the British Cabinet: 'Relief is perfectly possible, but the military authorities in Cape Town will do nothing.'

Lord Methuen's sharp rebuff at Magersfontein during 'Black Week' had the effect of pulling Rhodes up short. Clearly the relief of   97

𝔙. 𝔕.

OWNERS OF HORSES and MULES

Suitable for slaughtering purposes are invited to bring them to the Washington Market on **TUESDAYS** and **FRIDAYS** at 12 noon. A good price for fat animals.

The amount agreed upon at the time of purchase will be paid out every Thursday morning, between the hours of 9.30 and 11.30, at the Town Hall.

By order,

H. V. GORLE, Major,
Army Service Corps.

Kimberley, January 26, 1900. .   a1250

Kimberley would be a longer business than he had imagined. Christmas came, and with it a message, carried in its last stages by a runner, from Queen Victoria: 'I wish you and all my brave soldiers a happy Christmas. God protect and bless you all.'

The Boers began to bombard the town heavily – though inconsistently. In reply, the de Beers' workshops built a big gun, with a 4·1-inch bore and able to fire a 28-pound shell. Affectionately and inevitably nicknamed 'Long Cecil', its shell cases stamped with the message 'With C.J.R's Comps.', the gun began to roar out its daily defiance at the besiegers. Long Cecil was in action from the middle of January, at which time Colonel Kekewich reckoned that his ammunition, food supply and forage would last out until 28 February.

But on 7 February, with morale in Kimberley already low, provisions running out, and relief still some way off, the Boers began to shell the town with the Long Tom that had been damaged at the siege of Ladysmith and subsequently repaired in Pretoria. The huge shells screeched into Kimberley's residential quarters, killing and maiming a good many civilians, including women and children.

Long Tom began to terrorize the town's defenders, and desperate efforts were made to dig appropriate shelters. In an attempt to cut down casualties, Kekewich devised an early warning system: a signaller on the watchtower waved a flag whenever he saw Long Tom's puff of smoke four miles away, then buglers situated throughout the town sounded the alarm, and the townspeople had approximately fifteen seconds to take cover. Though this system naturally lacked the efficiency of modern radar and early warning techniques, it undoubtedly saved some lives.

This most recent hazard, however, was too much for Cecil Rhodes, especially with Lord Roberts's relief column inactive a few miles away on the Modder River. He let the Mayor of Kimberley and Kekewich know that he would call a public meeting unless he was informed, within forty-eight hours, of the precise and definite plans to relieve the town. Kekewich was appalled at this ultimatum, believing that Rhodes would persuade the public meeting to surrender Kimberley to the Boers. Rhodes, indeed, spelled out his intentions to Kekewich by shouting: 'Before Kimberley surrenders I will take good care that the English people know what I think of all this.'

Kekewich at once informed Lords Roberts and Methuen of the situation by heliograph. Roberts replied, urging patience, and Kekewich, encouraged at having the new commander-in-chief so near at hand, heliographed back on 9 February 1900:

> Will do my best but fear will have great difficulty restraining Rhodes and others from precipitating matters. Rhodes informed me today he would call a meeting in two days' time unless definite information column movements given him. Can forbid meeting but difficulty in preventing same his influence here so great. He is quite unreasonable. Shelling here severe and causing great alarm.

Rhodes kept up the pressure for a speedy relief. On 10 February the scanty Kimberley newspaper the *Diamond Fields Advertiser* carried a vehement article entitled 'Why Kimberley Cannot Wait', which was more or less unadulterated Rhodes:

> After the disturbing events of the last three days, we think it must have been brought home to Lord Roberts and to the whole world that, in the interests of humanity, the relief of this beleaguered city can no longer be delayed. How utterly the public and the authorities have failed to grasp the claim which Kimberley, by the heroic exertions of her citizens, has established upon the British Empire is only too apparent ... the utter indifference with which our fate appears to be regarded by the military hierarchy. Yet what are the facts? We have stood a siege which is rapidly approaching the duration of the Siege of Paris; we have

practically defended ourselves with citizen soldiers ... and through the genius of Mr Labram we have been able not merely to supply ammunition for the pop-guns sent to Kimberley, but also to produce in our own workshops the only weapon capable of minimizing the terrible havoc and destruction caused by the enemy's six-inch gun ... Although the difficulties of getting news have been almost insuperable, we are fully aware there are at the present moment 120,000 British troops in South Africa ... Arrayed against this vast Army – the largest by far that England has ever got together since the Napoleonic wars – are the burghers of two small republics ... and why in the name of common sense should Kimberley wait? ... Military men may make maps at the War Office, and may chatter in Cape Town; they may continue to evolve the most wonderful schemes and plans to take the place of those which one by one they have had to abandon, but they cannot, save at the risk of jeopardizing the whole campaign, evade the task of relieving Kimberley. [Magersfontein] is said to be an impregnable position, but what of that? There is a way into Kimberley over perfectly flat country ... We have held our tongues for long, believing that relief was merely a question of days, or at most a week. We have now reached a situation when either a newspaper must speak out or it has no *raison d'être*, and should cease to exist. They shout to us 'Have patience'. Will they remember that we have fought alone and unaided for four long months? Will they remember that we are situated practically in the centre of a desert 600 miles from the coast? ... Is it unreasonable, when our women and children are being slaughtered, and our buildings fired, to expect something better than that a large British Army should remain inactive in the presence of eight or ten thousand peasant soldiers.

Kekewich, enraged at the way in which the article broke censorship and revealed military information, ordered the editor's arrest. But Cecil Rhodes had prudently hidden the editor down a diamond mine, and Kekewich had to be content with closing down the newspaper. Kekewich was also determined that Rhodes should not call his threatened public meeting. Instead the latter held a smaller meeting with twelve of Kimberley's leading citizens, and then went to Kekewich and demanded that the statement drawn up by the meeting should be immediately sent to Roberts over the heliograph. Kekewich told Rhodes that the signallers were working under great pressure and would not be able to send the message for some time. At this Rhodes flew into a violent rage, and hurled himself at Kekewich shouting 'You low, damned, mean cur'. Not content with upbraiding the colonel in the tones of a G. A. Henty hero, Rhodes also tried to punch him in the face. Fortunately the Mayor of Kimberley, who was present, intervened and prevented the two men coming to blows. Rhodes then stormed off, with the mayor at his heels.

Rhodes's message was as follows:

On behalf of the inhabitants of these towns, we respectfully desire to be
informed whether there is any intention on your part to make an
immediate effort for our relief. Your troops have been for more than two
months within a distance of little over twenty miles from Kimberley ...
Scurvy is rampant among the natives; children, owing to a lack of
proper food, are dying in great numbers, and dysentery and typhoid
are very prevalent. The chief food of the whites has been bread and
horsemeat for a long time past ... a six-inch gun is daily causing death
among the population ... It is absolutely essential that immediate relief
should be afforded to this place.

Kekewich duly flashed an abbreviated version of this message to
Lord Roberts on the Modder River. Within an hour Roberts had
sent his reply telling Kekewich to arrest anyone, no matter how

illustrious, if they were a danger to security. Roberts at the same time sent encouraging words to Rhodes and his fellow leading citizens:

> I beg you to represent to the Mayor and Rhodes as strongly as you possibly can disastrous and humiliating effect of surrendering after so prolonged and glorious defence. Many days cannot possibly pass before Kimberley will be relieved, as we commence active operations tomorrow. Our further military operations depend in a large degree on your maintaining your position a very short time longer.

Soon all Kimberley knew that the relief force would start operations the next day (11 February 1900). Rhodes was partly placated, though he drafted a strongly worded reply to Roberts, which ended, 'It is high time you did something.' Colonel Kekewich refused to relay this message, which he considered to be offensive, and Rhodes subsequently sent a milder, though still forceful, one.

For his part, Kekewich wrote to Roberts trying to explain why Rhodes and he had clashed so dramatically. He wrote: 'Rhodes during the siege has done excellent work. And also, when his views on military questions have coincided with mine, he has readily assisted me, but he desires to control the military situation. I have refused to be dictated to by him. On such occasions he has been grossly insulting ... I have put up with insults so as not to risk the safety of the defence.'

On 11 February, with most of the women, children and civilian males crammed into the galleries of de Beers' mines, the defenders of Kimberley knew that the nearby British forces were moving to their relief. Looking south towards Jacobsdal and the Magersfontein Hills, observers could see a huge column of dust or smoke in the sky. Perhaps it was rising from the tumult of a great battle, or from the movement of thousands of troops. At any rate, it was coming northwards towards them.

Mafeking was a small border town situated at the junction of three territories – Cape Colony, the Bechuanaland Protectorate and the South African Republic (the Transvaal). The Western Railway line, that started in Cape Town and reached Bulawayo in Rhodesia, passed through Mafeking, thus giving it some strategic significance. Arguably, however, the Boers were mistaken in committing a large force to its encirclement, but for them, as for the British, Mafeking became a symbolic prize, squeezed between conflicting interests. It

Baden-Powell, hero of
Mafeking, immortalized
upon a patriotic plate.

was a neat, new little town of some fifteen hundred white inhabitants,
built round a spacious market square; it had the Victoria Hospital,
a convent, the railway station, a racecourse, a recreation ground, a
bank, a library, a courthouse, a gaol, hotels, schools, churches,
shops, and a masonic hall. It was not unlike scores of small towns in
southern Africa, yet it was destined to endure a siege of 217 days.

In July 1899 Colonel R. S. S. Baden-Powell arrived in South
Africa and was sent to the north-west Cape to raise and train two
regiments of mounted infantry, and to take charge of the defence of
that area and of Bechuanaland and Rhodesia. He had successfully
raised his troops, and garnered up some units from the Bechuanaland Police and from Rhodesia's British South African Police force,
by the time war broke out on 12 October. In all, Baden-Powell had
745 soldiers under his command – too few to take on the Boers in the
field. He therefore withdrew to Mafeking and prepared to defend it
against the enemy forces invading the north-west Cape.

Inside Mafeking, Baden-Powell mustered 450 citizens as volunteers, but this only meant that in all he had some twelve hundred   103

Alarm Bell ↑

Bombproof covered with
Tarpaulin ↑

Traverse of hay
bales ↑

HEADQUARTERS OFFICE, MAFEKING, NOVEMBER 12, 1899

HEADQUARTERS OFFICE : BOMB-PROOF

men to defend the town against Piet Cronje's nine thousand Transvaalers. Baden-Powell was also short of guns: he had four muzzle-loading 7-pounders, two small quick firers, a ¾-pounder Nordenfeld, a 1-pounder Hotchkiss, and seven Maxim guns. The Boers had at least ten modern pieces of artillery, and towards the end of October 1899 a 94-pounder Creusot. The great Creusot siege gun could hurl its heavy shell right into the centre of Mafeking; the Afrikaners nicknamed it 'Marguerit', then 'Gretchen'; the British called it 'Old Creaky'.

The defences of Mafeking stretched in a five-mile perimeter encompassing the European township, a small village occupied by Fingos, and a large settlement of the Barolong people at Mafikeng (the Place of Rocks). The fortifications, which had to be constructed hastily when hostilities broke out, connected a series of small forts of which the two most formidable were Cannon Kopje (in the south) and Fort Ayr (in the north-west). Apart from these fortifications, and his antiquated guns, Baden-Powell had plenty of dynamite. He ordered that mines should be made by filling wooden boxes with dynamite; the boxes were then placed at various points on the defensive perimeter and connected by wires to his headquarters next to Dixon's Hotel in the centre of the town. In fact, most of the boxes were filled with sand, but several genuine mines were detonated to impress the Boers and their spies within the defences. This largely fictitious mine network apparently did have a deterrent effect on the besieging Boers. Underground shelters were also dug for the women and children, and Baden-Powell tried to ensure that the citizens were given early warning whenever Old Creaky fired.

Baden-Powell's defence of Mafeking became a legend cherished throughout the Empire, and even beyond. Autocratic, imaginative, firm-minded, humorous, and on occasion ruthless, Baden-Powell came to symbolize 'British pluck' at a time when British power looked fallible if not ludicrously inadequate. Under his direction, the improvisations of Mafeking's defenders were impressive. The railway staff constructed an armoured train out of freight trucks by fixing spare rails horizontally down the sides of the trucks, leaving gaps as loopholes. An old cannon was dug up; it turned out to be a 1770 bronze ship's gun, bearing the propitious letters B.P. on its breech; it was transformed in the railway workshops into a workable piece of artillery, named 'Lord Nelson', and able to fire some three thousand yards. Another gun was actually manufactured in the workshops, and proved able to throw its homemade 18-pound shell a distance of four thousand yards, thus making it the most powerful gun inside Mafeking.

Opposite Baden-Powell's sketches of the bomb-proof headquarters at Mafeking, November 1899.

His activities in Mafeking also helped to advance Baden-Powell's ideas on scouting. Before the siege he had written a book, *Aids to Scouting*, which described scouting techniques for soldiers. Once the siege was under way, he got Major Lord Edward Cecil (son of Lord Salisbury, the British Prime Minister) to set up the Mafeking Cadet Corps. This organization was made up of boys aged between nine and fifteen, dressed in khaki, with forage caps. They acted as postmen and messengers. Baden-Powell later wrote: 'The possibility of putting responsibility onto boys and treating them seriously was brought to proof in Mafeking with the corps of boys raised by Lord Edward Cecil there in 1899 and led me to go into it further.' So, in a very real sense, the world scouting movement grew out of a battle for supremacy in southern Africa.

The siege was, on the whole, conducted along honourable lines. Baden-Powell agreed with Cronje that there should be no belligerent activity on Sundays; nor should there be any firing on the mule-drawn ambulances flying the red cross, the convent, the Victoria Hospital, or the camp that was eventually established outside the town for women and children. When these understandings were violated, the two sides tended to engage in a lengthy correspondence. Within Mafeking, Baden-Powell quickly replaced civil law with martial law, under which some stern (perhaps too stern) sentences were meted out in the interests of security.

The Boer 'Long Tom' siege gun outside Mafeking.

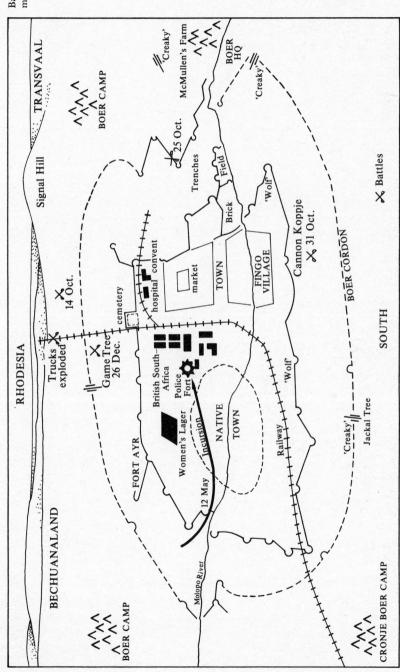

RHODESIA

BECHUANALAND

TRANSVAAL

Signal Hill

BOER CAMP

BOER CAMP

CRONJE BOER CAMP

'Creaky'

McMullen's Farm

BOER HQ

'Creaky'

25 Oct.

Trenches

Brick Field

'Wolf'

Cannon Koppie
31 Oct.

BOER CORDON

SOUTH

Battles

14 Oct.

cemetery

hospital convent

market

TOWN

FINGO VILLAGE

Trucks exploded

Game Tree
26 Dec.

British South Africa Police Fort

Women's Lager

FORT AYR

Incursion

12 May

NATIVE TOWN

'Wolf'

Railway

'Creaky'

Jackal Tree

Molopo River

Some defenders of
Mafeking stand
proudly by their home-
made cannon.

Apart from the artillery duel, and the occasional skirmish, there
were few serious clashes between the two sides. On 31 October 1899,
however, the Boers did launch a determined attack on Cannon
Kopje, but were successfully rebuffed. Soloman Plaatje, the African
interpreter to the Mafeking court, wrote a wry account of this
attack and its prelude:

Monday, 30th [October]
During this day we received another ultimatum that if we did not
surrender we would be bombarded early next day. We knew that the
big gun had been with us for more than a week and as she failed to
shake us in eight days I am afraid that the Boers are merely fooling

themselves to imagine that we entertain any fear in being bombarded – for so far from being alarmed, we are getting used to it. I look back to reflect on the slight damage caused by these shells, nearly 200 of which have already been wasted on the town. Considering the expense of one of them (opinion on this point differs, some saying £35 and some £47), she is really not worth the fuss. Meanwhile the position of the big commando at Lothlakane is being moved down the river to a spot about three miles west of here, and one from the eastern to another spot three miles to the north. We are anxiously waiting to see what tomorrow's day will bring forth.

Tuesday, 31st

Long before 5 o'clock we were aroused by reports of Ben [the Creusot 94-pounder] going as rapidly as she did last week. She was accompanied by the enemy's 7-pounder and all other pounders. We woke, dressed in a hurry, and went to the rocks to find things really very serious at Makane. They were shelling Makane and the dust was simply like a cloud around our little fort. The Boers were advancing towards the koppie like a swarm of voetgangers [wingless locusts]: they came creeping under cover of their shells, which were flying over their heads and preceding them like a lot of lifeless but terrific vanguards, until they opened fire with their muskets at long range. Their fire was very heavy, for the whole of the Dutch army had come over from all round Mafeking and turned their attention towards our little fort at Makane. They have evidently discovered that to capture the whole place at once was a hopeless task and they had therefore decided on capturing one by one of our forts until they have nipped every one of them in the bud …

To return to the subject. I think I have already stated that the Boers attributed their failure to the fact that we never leave our trenches to give them a chance of tackling us in the open: this morning they must have thought that they would easily compel us to do so by weakening Makane and naturally getting us to run to her assistance, thereby affording them an opportunity of going for us in the plain between this and there. If this was their expectation they were sorely disappointed, for nobody cared. They went for the little fort from east, south and west with muskets and artillery, the former being volleys from about 800 hands. But nobody in town, or anywhere else, troubled his soul about it. The volunteers round the place, seeing that all of the guns were turned towards Makane, stood up and admired the operation as though it was a performance on a theatre stage. It must have given them a headache to find such a multitude of them advancing towards a fort occupied by 70 officers and men of the B.S.A. Police – and nobody caring to go to their assistance. But this was not all: the enemy came quite close and still not a shot came from within the mysterious little fort. I believe the Boers (who always let off a number of rounds unnecessarily) must have thought that everyone was dead, for nearly 20 tons of bombs had already been plugged into the fort. The fortifications looked quite old and ragged in consequence. All of a sudden there came volley after volley from the dumb fort and we could see them fall when the Maxim began to play; some dead, some wounded, and some presumably to wait until dark … Our losses were 2 officers and 5 men killed, and 6 wounded.

Shortly after Christmas, the British also made an attack upon Game Tree Fort. The armoured train opened fire, two 7-pounders blazed away, and two squadrons of troops attacked the fort in extended line. But the Boers had been forewarned of the attack by spies and they shot down their attackers, killing twenty-four. This was the heaviest loss the defenders suffered during the siege.

The siege continued. Baden-Powell's main problems were food supplies and keeping up morale. There were sufficient provisions to last the Europeans until the end of April 1900, but the Barolongs were less fortunate, caught as they were in this 'white man's war'. There was insufficient pasture for the Barolongs' cattle, and no mealies to crop. Baden-Powell set up soup kitchens, and later explained how horses were shot and utilized:

> When a horse was killed, his mane and tail were cut off and sent to the hospital for stuffing mattresses and pillows. His shoes went to the foundry for making shells. His skin after having the hair scalded off, was boiled with his head and feet for many hours, chopped up small, and ... served as 'brawn'.
>
> His flesh was taken from the bones and minced in a great mincing machine and from his inside were made skins into which the meat was crammed and each man received a sausage as his ration.
>
> The bones were then boiled into rich soup, which was dealt out at the different soup kitchens; and they were afterwards pounded into powder with which to adulterate the flour.

Not only horses were eaten by the besieged Africans. A barely palatable porridge was made out of the husks of forage oats; locusts were raked up and devoured; stray dogs were also shot and eaten. The markedly different rations available to Europeans and Africans emphasized commonplace racial assumptions in southern Africa.

Baden-Powell was adept at keeping morale high. For example he posted a casualty list outside his headquarters which read:

> *Killed:* one hen
> *Wounded:* one yellow dog
> *Smashed:* one hotel window

But when Kimberley and Ladysmith had been relieved, and the British under Roberts and Kitchener were pressing triumphantly into the Orange Free State and towards Pretoria, the citizens of Mafeking began to feel aggrieved. On 30 March 1900 Baden-Powell published a warm rejoinder to the jeremiahs and rumour-mongers in the *Mafeking Mail*:

I hear that again wiseacres are busy in town, informing people as to what I am doing and what I am leaving undone. As their deductions are somewhat inaccurate I wish to state that the condition of affairs is in no way altered by my last general notice, which stated we must be prepared to remain besieged all that time. Indeed I hope that we may be free within the next fortnight or three weeks, but it would be folly on our part not to be prepared against possible unforeseen delays. Had we not been thus prepared in the first instance we should all have been prisoners in Pretoria by the beginning of January, and the Boers would have now been enjoying the use of our property in Mafeking.

I am, I suppose, the most anxious of anybody in Mafeking to see a Relief Column here and the siege at an end; all that can be done for our relief, from both North and South, is being done, but the moves of troops in the face of the enemy must necessarily be slow, and we have to sit in patience until they develop.

As regards the smallness of our rations, we could, of course, live well on full rations for a week or two and then give in to the 'women slaughter-ers' and let them take their vengeance on the town, whereas by limiting our amount of daily food we can make certain of outlasting all their efforts against us. The present ration, properly utilised, is a fairly full one as compared with those issued in other sieges – in fact I and my staff have, during the past few days, been living on a far smaller ration with-out any kind of extras to improve it – and we still live.

There are, by the way, two hints I should like to give for making small rations go further – hints derived from personal experience of previous hungry times – and these are:–

1. To lump your rations together as much as possible for cooking, and not every man to have his little amount cooked separately.

2. To make the whole into a big thick stew, from which, even three quarter lb. of ingredients per man, three good meals can be got per day.

It is just possible that we may have to take 2 oz. off the bread stuffs, but otherwise our supplies will last well over the period indicated. It has been objected that we are feeding horses on oats, but the oats so used are a lot (of Colonial oats) that have been found quite useless for making flour from for human consumption.

I am told that I keep back news from the public. This is not in accordance with facts, for I make a point of publishing all news of general interest as soon as possible after receipt, first by telephone, then by notices posted about, and lastly through Mr Whales, in the Mafeking Mail Slips; I have no object whatever in keeping news back. Occasion-ally, of course, items of military information have to be kept quiet because, as we all know, their publication in Mafeking means their transmission within a few hours, to the enemy's camp ...

I am always, not only willing, but anxious to personally hear any reasonable complaints or suggestions, and those who have them to make, need only bring their grievances to me to get what redress is in my power, but veiled hints and growlings cannot be permitted; at such times as these they are apt to put people 'on edge' and to alarm the

Soldiers of the Queen. Queen Victoria visits her wounded troops at the Herbert Hospital,
Woolwich, March 1900.

ladies, and for these reasons they must be suppressed. 'Grousing' is generally the outcome of funk on the part of the individual who grouses, and I hope that every right-minded man who hears any of it will shut it up with an appropriate remark, or the toe of his boot. Cavillers should keep quiet until the siege is over and then they are welcome to write or talk until they are blue in the face.

Still, Britain, and indeed the Empire, waited anxiously for Mafeking's relief. Amid his tribulations Baden-Powell may have taken some comfort from a message from Queen Victoria sent in 1900 saying: 'I continue watching with confidence and admiration in the patient and resolute defence which is so gallantly maintained under your ever resourceful command. V.R.I.'

Chapter 7

Lord Roberts to the Rescue

On 10 February Lord Roberts, encamped on the Modder, summoned his senior officers and said:

I have asked General French to call you together as I want to tell you that I am going to give you some very hard work to do, but at the same time you are to get the greatest chance cavalry has ever had. I am certain you will do well ... You will remember what you are going to do all your lives, and when you have grown to be old men you will tell the story of the relief of Kimberley. My intention is for you to make a detour and get on the railway north of the town. The enemy are afraid of the British cavalry, and I hope that when you get them into the open you will make an example of them.

Roberts had decided on a bold stroke against the enemy: he was all too aware of Rhodes's and Kekewich's quarrel at Kimberley; further east, in northern Cape Colony, Generals Schoeman and de la Rey were poised to harry his communications; he knew, moreover, that in north Natal Buller had once more failed to relieve Ladysmith.

Though short of fit horses, and with his organization incomplete, Roberts put his faith in speed and surprise. Basically, he planned to move south from the Modder River camp to Ramdan, a town to the east of Graspan station – where Lord Methuen had earlier fought a successful minor battle. His forces would then sweep eastwards to cross the Riet River, and would next press northwards, on Cronje's east flank, and ford the Modder River. Once across the Modder, General French would surge forward to the relief of Kimberley; Roberts would then decide whether to support French in the west or make for Bloemfontein, capital of the Orange Free State.

Cronje did not apparently suspect that he was about to be out-flanked. Shortly after midnight, in the early hours of 11 February, the British forces began to move off; there were 25,000 infantry, nearly 8,000 cavalry and mounted infantry, more than 100 guns, and thousands of supply wagons. In order to deceive the Boers, French's cavalry, which was the first to move, left all their tents standing. By daybreak the whole column was uncoiling, making for Ramdan, which was the only watering place before the Riet River.

As French's troops approached the fords of the Riet, Cronje and de Wet struggled to interpret Lord Roberts's intentions. At first de Wet thought the cavalry were going to raid Faursmith thirty miles to the east; then Jacobsdal, just north of the Riet, seemed a likely objective. By 13 February Cronje was none the wiser as to his enemy's strategy. By this time, the main force, with its supply wagons, had reached the Riet where a confused pile-up of wagons

Opposite Relieved at last! Buller's men march into Ladysmith after its long ordeal.

ensued until Lord Kitchener diverted some of the columns to another ford.

At last French was able to lead off his six thousand horsemen, with all their supplies, ammunition, forty-two guns, and a cart which unwound telegraph wire as it went. De Wet, grossly outnumbered, made no attempt to intercept this force, though he reported its progress to Cronje who said to the messenger, a Cape rebel named Scheepers, 'Are you afraid of things like that? Just you go and shoot them down, and catch them when they run.'

There was, however, no chance of shooting down French and his men. By the early afternoon of 13 February he was nearing the Modder River, and though harassed by a small enemy force on his right he went through the textbook manoeuvre of turning his horsemen half-right and thus edged his way towards the river. When the green banks of the Modder came in sight, the whole cavalry force wheeled towards the river and galloped for the crossing. A few Boers were scattered, and the British troops forded the river.

A vital stage of the operation had now been reached, though at the cost of five hundred dead or unfit horses. The British cavalry held Klip Drift and Rondavel Drift; French's men made full use of abandoned Boer wagons of food, and fed their exhausted horses on forage left behind in the enemy's laagers; the Modder quenched the thirst of man and beast alike. It was now a question of waiting for the rest of the force to arrive so that the infantry could guard the drifts across the Modder and allow the cavalry to make for Kimberley.

Two days later the infantry and wagons plodded to the banks of the Modder. General Kitchener, the Chief of Staff, arrived to supervise the rear, while French prepared for the final ride to Kimberley. He set out at 8.30 a.m. on 15 February. General Cronje, now realizing with dismay that he had been outflanked, was determined, with de Wet, to put up some sort of opposition to French's forces. The Boers thus took up strong positions on two conjoining ridges to the north of Klip Drift. There were about eight hundred men, and two guns. As French's men rode towards the ridges they came under shell fire, but the British artillery was turned on the Boers and their guns were silenced.

French now decided to force his way between the two ridges and out into the open country beyond. If he succeeded Kimberley would certainly be relieved within hours. The stage was now set for one of the last great cavalry charges of history. With the 9th and 16th Lancers leading, wave after wave of horsemen galloped into the valley between the two ridges, pennants flying, lances and sabres

at the ready. A great cloud of dust billowed up from the horses' hooves, making it difficult for the Boers to aim properly. The British artillery kept firing until the last possible moment. The Boers broke and fled, leaving a score captured or speared. French had broken through with spectacular ease, and at the cost of seven dead and little more than thirty wounded.

After an hour's rest, French led his cavalry straight for Kimberley. The dispirited and panic-stricken Boers were reeling from the cavalry's success, and, to the west, staggering from the ferocious bombardment Lord Methuen had unleashed upon the Magersfontein Hills. Their opposition faded away.

Shortly after 4 p.m. a patrol of Australian Horse rode into Kimberley, and the townspeople emerged from the mine-shafts to cheer and gape. Towards evening General French arrived with the main body of the force. For the first time for months British arms had achieved a striking success, and the telegraph lines bore

The Royal Canadian Regiment cross the Paardeberg Drift in their bid to outflank Cronje.

the proud, and perhaps unexpected, message, 'Kimberley has been relieved'.

The *Daily Mail* was overjoyed, and said on 17 February: 'Kimberley is won, Mr Cecil Rhodes is free, the de Beers' shareholders are all full of themselves, and the beginning of the war is at an end. It is a great feat to have accomplished, and the happiest omen for the future. There is no one like Bobs!'

More soberly, the *New York Tribune* commented on 18 February: 'The relief of Kimberley and the retreat of Cronje have completely transformed the whole aspect of the war. The fighting is now transferred from British to Boer soil. The advance on Bloemfontein and Pretoria has actually begun and the investment of Ladysmith is likely to be abandoned. The Boers must relinquish their schemes of conquest and fall back in defence of their own territory.'

A cavalry officer, Major Edmund Allenby (later to achieve fame as Field-Marshal Allenby, the conqueror of Jerusalem in the Great War), wrote of the entry into Kimberley:

> We got in here after a very hard week. We are in a beastly bivouac, tentless, blanketless, unwashed and dusty. We lost about ten officers killed and wounded, and I think about thirty men. My property now consists of the dirty clothes I live and sleep in day and night, a cloak, a saddle blanket, a toothbrush, a box of cigarettes and a tube of lanoline. On the march I lived chiefly on biscuits and beef tongues. The horses are half-starved, Rhodes is behaving very well. He sent over some soup, firewood, etc. I dined with him last night. He's much the same as I remember him fifteen years ago ... Last week was the longest week I ever spent. It feels like six months.

As to the conditions which the relieving forces found at Kimberley, a war correspondent wrote:

> What one noticed first was the number of holes and shelters and warrens into which people had crept for safety. Hundreds of them, like human ant-hills ... The menu at the principal hotel, where I dined, would (if it had been printed) have consisted of one item – horseflesh. I noticed that the residents ate it eagerly, and even talked about it; but most of us strangers arose hungry and went quickly into the fresh air ... One found man after man thin, listless and (in spite of the joy of salvation) dispirited; talking with a tired voice and hopeless air, and with a queer, shifty, nervous, scared look in the eye ... The thing was scarcely human, scarcely of this world. These men were not like oneself ... All this fear and horror to be borne upon an empty stomach, for the horrors of partial starvation were added to the constant fear of a violent death. Mothers had to see their babies die because there was no milk or other suitable nourishment; a baby cannot live on horse and mule flesh. There was hardly a coloured baby left alive.

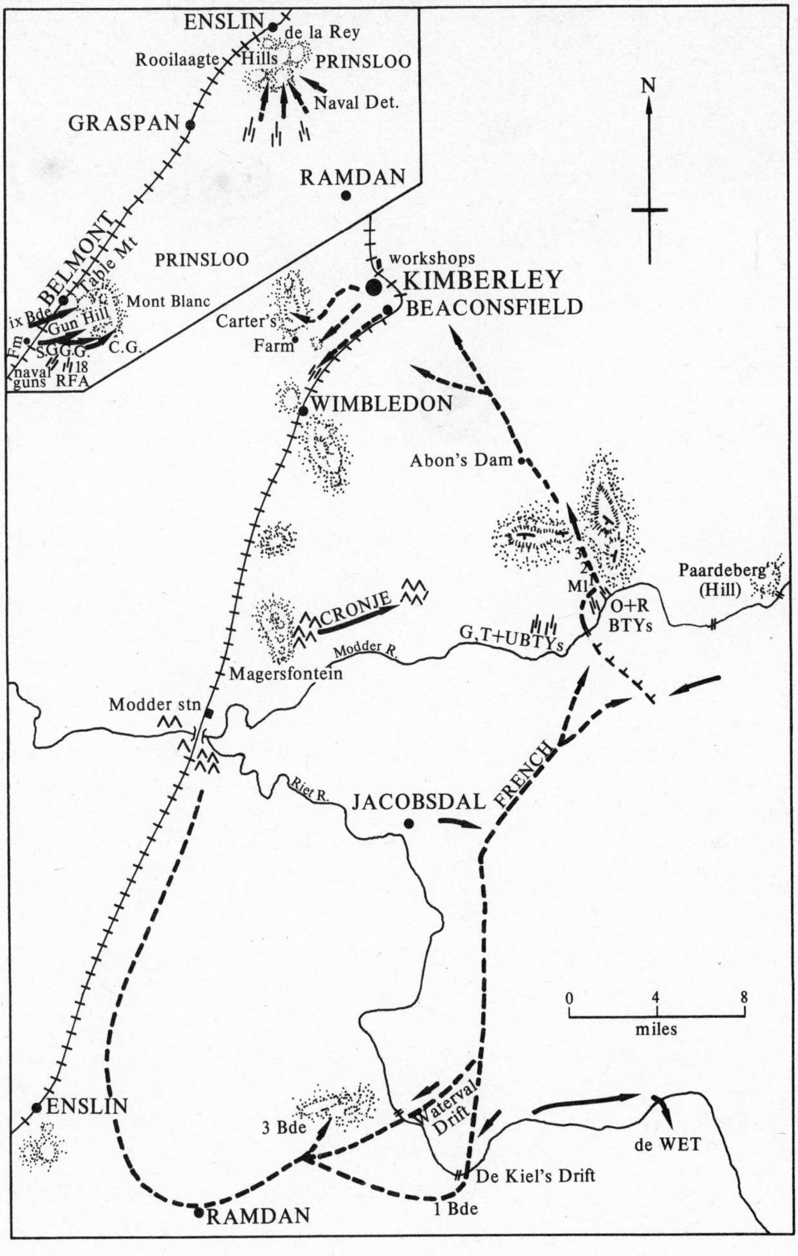
ENSLIN
de la Rey
Rooilaagte
Hills
PRINSLOO
Naval Det.
GRASPAN
RAMDAN
N
BELMONT
Table Mt
PRINSLOO
Mont Blanc
ix Bde
Gun Hill
C.G.
S.G.G.
Fm
naval guns
18 RFA
workshops
KIMBERLEY
BEACONSFIELD
Carter's Farm
WIMBLEDON
Abon's Dam
3
2
MI
Paardeberg (Hill)
O+R BTYs
CRONJE
G.T+U BTYs
Modder R.
Magersfontein
Modder stn
Riet R.
JACOBSDAL
FRENCH
0
4
8
miles
ENSLIN
3 Bde
Waterval Drift
De Kiel's Drift
1 Bde
RAMDAN
de WET

The relief of Kimberley, February 1900, including the earlier battles of Belmont and Graspan. Klip Drift is shown where French's cavalry crossed the Modder (not named).

With Kimberley relieved, General Cronje's will to resist temporarily crumbled. He sat in his laager as if paralysed, with Methuen's guns roaring in the distance. His wife, more indomitable than he, sought to comfort him by patting his head. At last he shook off his lethargy and despair, and considered what to do. He could not go north since French held Kimberley; to the south was Methuen; to the west was barren wasteland. Although the main British force was marching up from the south-east, there was still a gap through which he could slip eastwards towards Bloemfontein.

Before midnight on 15 February Cronje's army abandoned the Magersfontein Hills and made off to the east. There were about five thousand men, many wives and children, four hundred wagons and several thousand horses. By the time dawn broke on 16 February Cronje had got away, though an infantry division and a brigade of mounted infantry, urged on by the relentless Kitchener, snapped at his heels as he crossed the Modder.

After their success in relieving Kimberley, the British forces faced some frustrations. Roberts failed to get a message to French ordering him to block Cronje's retreat, because the Boers had cut the telegraph wires. French himself pursued the main Afrikaner force, under J. S. Ferreira, that had been besieging Kimberley, and was now making off northwards, dragging their Creusot siege gun, but failed to run them down; his horses were desperate for water, the Boers fought a brisk rearguard, and the chase was abandoned. Worse still, de Wet, with about a thousand men, swooped onto the great British supply park at Waterval on the north bank of the Riet and swept aside all resistance. Roberts decided to abandon the supply park so as not to slow down his advance by turning back to fight for it; but four days' supplies were lost, and the men were on short rations for some time.

Roberts now ordered all available forces to pursue Cronje's convoy. On 17 February French, who could only muster twelve hundred sound horses, set off to intercept Cronje and bar his retreat until the main British force caught up with him. The Boer column pressed on. They did not know that Kitchener was pushing the infantry along behind them with forced marches, nor that Sir John French was bearing down on them from the north-west.

Shortly before noon Cronje's army prepared to cross to the south bank of the Modder to get onto the Bloemfontein road; they had just passed a hill called Paardeberg on the north bank of the river. The wagons halted while the midday meal was prepared. It must have seemed to the Boers that they had virtually made their escape, with the British infantry struggling along in their rear.

Suddenly, without any warning, a salvo of shells crashed among them. Panic followed, as men, women and children desperately sought shelter. French's guns had opened up. He had slogged to his present position on a line of hills called the Koedoesrand, north-east of Cronje, in seven hours, and on Roberts' orders. The Boers were, for the moment, a sitting target.

French was not wholly comfortable, however. Cronje's force outnumbered his by nearly five to one; furthermore, Ferreira's men, retreating from Kimberley, might come up upon his rear at any moment. He anxiously scanned the western skyline. At last he could see large forces approaching to within two and a half miles of the Boer positions. It was Kitchener, who had driven the infantry along for a thirty-mile march, mostly under a burning sun, and who had accomplished the feat within twenty-four hours. Roberts, mean-while, had fallen ill at Jacobsdal, but had confirmed Kitchener in command (a decision which reduced the more senior General Kelly-Kenny, the commander of the 6th Division, to a mood of sulky, limited co-operation).

Cronje was trapped. As night fell he decided to stand and fight rather than try to escape. He had five thousand men, and had sent for further reinforcements from Bloemfontein; General Ferreira was nearby with 1,500 troops, and de Wet, with a similar force, was closing in from the south.

The Battle of Paardeberg opened early in the morning of 18 February. Kitchener was determined to smash Cronje's army and inflict heavy losses upon it, in contrast to General Kelly-Kenny who suggested a leisurely bombardment and waiting for the enemy to surrender. This was not Kitchener's way at all; it was not for a gentlemanly joust that he had force-marched his sweat-soaked regiments of foot to Paardeberg; here was a notoriously elusive foe in a trap, and he was determined to move in for the kill. He surveyed the Boer positions through field glasses and decided to order an immediate attack.

Cronje's laager was north of the Modder, surrounded by trenches and set among trees; on the dry river bed below were sheltered the ox wagons, and the women and children. Two miles to the west of the main laager, there was a formidable defensive position in a donga (gully); on the other side of the laager there were more posts, stretching for three miles eastwards and capable of pouring out a deadly low trajectory fire. Kitchener's headquarters were two miles 121

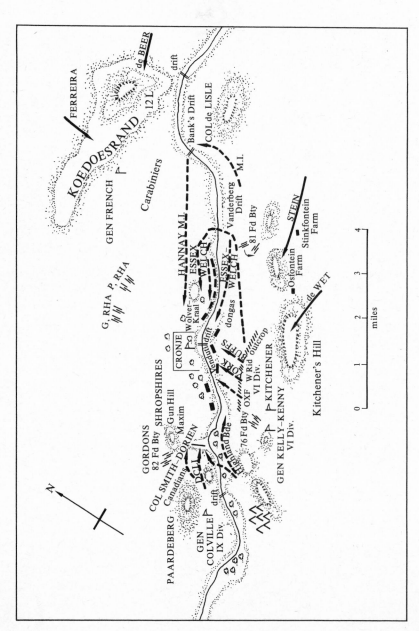

The Battle of
Paardeberg.

due south of Cronje's laager. He was confident of success, and as the main action began said to his staff officers, 'It is now seven o'clock. We shall be in the laager at half past ten, then I'll load up French and send him on to Bloemfontein.'

Kitchener's divisional commanders were not so optimistic. Kelly-Kenny was still resentful, and General Colville and Colonel Smith-Dorrien were by no means enthusiastic supporters of Kitchener's plan of attack. These, and other senior officers, were fearful that heavy casualties would result from a full-blooded assault on the Boer positions. It is likely that their views permeated their divisions and led to a certain half-heartedness in the approach of some units. For Kitchener there was no cause for hesitation. He planned to attack Cronje's laager from the east and the west and on both banks of the river; he also wanted a frontal attack to take place from the south.

The frontal attack from the south got off to a bad start and the troops were soon pinned down by accurate enemy rifle fire; casualties mounted steadily, and in the end the assault ground to a halt some three hundred yards from the river banks. In the east, and south of the river, the British forces were unexpectedly attacked in the rear by several hundred Boers, with two guns, come hot-foot from Bloemfontein, and led by Commandant Steyn. Although the British turned on Steyn, silenced his guns, and eventually drove him off the hills near Stinkfontein, large numbers of men were necessarily diverted from the pincer movement which Kitchener had planned. In the west, meanwhile, British troops attacked on both sides of the river; they made little progress, though two spirited attacks were made on the donga, first by Canadian forces and the Duke of Cornwall's Light Infantry together, and then by the Canadians alone.

Amid this turmoil, General Cronje sat holding his wife's hand, while shells landed among his wagons, and rifle fire crackled around him; he seemed calm, and gloomily fatalistic. Kitchener, on the other hand, positively exulted in the battle; but he lacked the staff to carry orders efficiently to the different units engaged in the struggle, and, as at Omdurman, spent a good deal of time galloping hither and thither issuing instructions to those officers nearest at hand.

By 10.30 a.m. precious little had been achieved, and British casualties were high. Kitchener now decided to throw in the mounted infantry, under Colonel Hannay, who had just driven off Steyn's Free Staters. The mounted infantry moved up and joined the Essex and Welch Regiments who had got to within eight hundred   123 yards of the main laager. Kitchener sent a curt message to Hannay, when the latter reported the progress he had made, saying, 'The time has now come for a final effort. All troops have been warned that the laager must be rushed at all costs. Try and carry the Essex and the Welch on with you. But if they cannot go, the M.I. should do it. Gallop up if necessary and fire into the laager.'

The risks of carrying out this implacable order were tremendous, but Hannay in a fit of adventure story bravado decided to attempt it. He gathered up a handful of men and rode straight towards the enemy; the Boers hesitated to shoot him down, so forlorn and mis-guided did he seem at the head of his men, but he came on relent-lessly and at last they had no alternative but to kill him. After Hannay's self-sacrifice, the Essex and Welch Regiments made an attempt to storm the laager, but were decisively checked by enemy fire. Almost simultaneously, the Cornwalls, the Canadians and the Highland Brigade launched another attack on the donga in the west; but the assault was ill co-ordinated, and Smith-Dorrien held back his reserves.

Everywhere British commanding officers were holding back. The light was fading fast, and they saw no point in amassing further casualties. De Wet, moreover, now created an awkward diversion by occupying Stinkfontein Farm and Kitchener's kopje, just to the east of Kitchener's headquarters; though he had only six hundred men, it took three days, and a foray by General French's cavalry, to drive him off.

As night fell, the Battle of Paardeberg ended. Both sides had fought themselves to a standstill. Though the British had suffered 1,262 casualties (more than on any other day throughout the war) they had had the best of it: Cronje was still penned within his laager, surrounded by over three hundred casualties and the corpses of many of his trek oxen; he had no doctors to tend his wounded; un-less substantial reinforcements arrived promptly he was doomed. Kitchener's abrupt assault on the laager had at least left no time for the Boers to wriggle out of the trap, and if his divisional com-manders had shown more enthusiasm for his ruthless tactics the day might have ended in a spectacular triumph for British arms.

The next day, 19 February, Lord Roberts arrived at Paardeberg, having shaken off his sickness. Disinclined himself to risk heavy casualties, he tactfully sent Kitchener to the rear to supervise the vital supply links. To the relief of most of his subordinates, Roberts decided upon an investment of the Boer positions. It is arguable that a further full-blooded assault would have settled matters within twenty-four hours, and would also have dealt the Boers such a

crippling blow in terms of casualties and morale that they would never have recovered. This did not happen. Even the British artillery bombardment was a desultory affair, though aided by an observation balloon overhead. The enemy, however, were unable to break out and escape.

On 26 and 27 February the British made two attempts to storm the laager. The assault troops came within 250 yards of their objective in the east, and within 550 yards in the west. Shortly after 6 a.m. on 27 February the Boers raised white flags. Cronje had accepted defeat.

Roberts immediately ordered a ceasefire. At 7 a.m. Cronje rode up to the British headquarters, where men of the Highland Brigade formed a hollow square. Lord Roberts greeted him cordially, shaking his hand and saying, 'I am glad to see you. You have made a gallant defence, sir.' Cronje, face to face with the realities of his failure, made no reply. The contrast between the appearance of the two commanders reflected their respective fortunes: Roberts was clad in a well tailored khaki uniform, unadorned save for the jewelled Kandahar sword at his side; Cronje wore an old, bulky, green overcoat, a slouch hat, and rough veldschoen boots.

A shabby and defeated General Cronje surrenders to Lord Roberts after the Battle of Paardeberg.

125

The defeated Boers stacked their arms upon the river bank, and were then led away into captivity; 2,500 Transvaalers and 1,500 Free Staters surrendered. Cronje and his wife were taken to Cape Town, though the vanquished commander was later shipped to St Helena (shades of Napoleon!) for safe keeping.

The victory at Paardeberg had great significance, much of it symbolic. In Britain there was relieved celebration, and brokers danced for joy in the London stock exchange. For the Boer republics the news came as a great blow, particularly since the surrender fell on the anniversary of their crushing victory at Majuba nineteen years before. 'The English,' Paul Kruger complained, 'have taken our Majuba Day away from us.' But this was not all, for the British had also decisively taken the initiative in the war. With Kimberley relieved, and the Boers falling back on Bloemfontein, the British were poised for a final breakthrough in north Natal.

General Buller had formulated yet one more plan for the relief of Ladysmith. Basically it consisted of a right-flanking movement which would drive the Boers off the group of hills dominated by Hlangwhane and within a great loop in the Tugela on the British side of the river. Buller had twenty-five thousand men with (as usual) ample food and supplies, and on 17 and 18 February a substantial part of this force drove about two thousand Boers off Hlangwhane and two nearby hills. As cautious as ever, Buller spent the next two days bringing up the rest of his army, while, to the west, Cronje was being brought to the point of surrender at Paardeberg.

Despite Buller's slow-footed advance, Boer morale sagged and many began to make for home. General Botha tried in vain to stop the rot, and in despair telegraphed to President Kruger that he feared the Tugela and even Ladysmith would have to be abandoned. Kruger replied in defiant vein, his exhortation owing much to the lessons of the Old Testament:

> The moment you cease to hold firm and fight in the name of the Lord, then you have unbelief in you; and the moment unbelief is present cowardice follows, and the moment that you turn your backs on the enemy then there remains no place for us to seek refuge, for in that case we have ceased to trust in the Lord. No, no, my brethren; let it not be so; let it not be so. Has not the Lord hitherto given us double proof that He stands on our side? Wherever our burghers have stood fast, however hard the task, the Lord has beaten back the enemy with a small number of our burghers. My brethren, is it not the same Lord that cleft the Red

Sea and routed Pharaoh and all his host, when Moses stood firm in his faith? Is it not, again, the same Lord that caused the stream of water to spring from the rocks whence thousands could drink? Is it not still the same Lord who walked on the sea and rebuked the waves of the sea and the winds, and they obeyed Him? ... It seems to me from a study of God's word that we live at a point of time spoken of in the Revelation, in which the Beast has received power to persecute the Church of Christ in order to purify her, as gold is purified through fire ... This, indeed, is the struggle for the crown, both in a material and a spiritual sense. Read Psalm XXVII, verse 7, where the Lord says, 'Be of good courage, little band of god-fearing ones.' The Lord is faithful, and in your weakness shall He make perfect His strength. Read Psalm XXXIII, verse 7, to the end, where it says that victory is in the hand of the Lord alone, and not with the multitude of horses and chariots ... No brethren, let us not bring all our posterity to destruction. Stand fast in faith to fight, and you shall be convinced that the Lord shall arise and shall scatter His enemies (Psalm LXVII). Our faith is now at its utmost test, but the Lord will now shortly prove that He alone lives and reigns. The young men preferred death in the fiery furnace to forsaking their faith. Our ancestors preferred the stake to abandoning their faith, and the Church has been preserved, and all those who have preferred death to forsaking their faith have been as a sacrifice on the altar. Read this out to all officers and burghers, and my faith and prayer lie in my firm confidence that the Lord shall strengthen His people in their faith. Even if they have no earthly rock behind which to seek cover, they shall win on the open plain.

Whether due to Kruger's stern rallying call or (more likely) to Buller's characteristically ponderous manoeuvres, the disintegration of Botha's forces was halted. By 21 February about five thousand Afrikaners were prepared to face the greatly superior numbers of their enemy. The British crossed the Tugela and marched northwards against a group of hills that included Horseshoe Hill, Hedge Hill and Terrace Hill. By 25 February the British forces were draped painfully across these hills, and subjected to an enfilading fire uncomfortably reminiscent of Spion Kop. But the 25th was also a Sunday and the Afrikaners were anxious for an armistice and a chance to tend the wounded and bury the dead. Buller was only too pleased to agree to this. On the Sunday British troops and Boers fraternized and exchanged gossip; one Afrikaner said to General Lyttelton, 'We've all been having a rough time,' to which Lyttelton replied stoically, 'Yes, I suppose so. But for us of course it's nothing. This is what we are paid for. This is the life we always lead – you understand?' 'Great God!' said the Boer, shocked.

During this pause in the operation, Buller, in consultation with General Warren, decided to alter his plans. He now proposed to bring back most of his force to the eastern bank of the Tugela, and

Overleaf The British storm Pieter's Hill and open the way for the Relief of Ladysmith.

then to launch, over a pontoon bridge, a three-pronged attack on the northern hills guarding the route, and the railway line, to Ladysmith; the attacking troops would be supported by artillery fire from seventy-six guns. The battle went better than Buller expected. His forces attacked along a three-mile front, concentrating on Pieter's Hill, Railway Hill and the still partially occupied Terrace Hill. The Boers were overwhelmed by the textbook assault of British troops, infantry and artillery working in close co-ordination.

Deneys Reitz, who was on Pieter's Hill, later described the attack in his book *Commando*:

> [the crest of Pieter's Hill was] almost invisible under the clouds of flying earth and fumes, while the volume of sound was beyond anything that I have ever heard. At intervals the curtain lifted, letting us catch a glimpse of trenches above, but we could see no sign of movement, nor could we hear if the men up there were still firing, for the din of guns drowned all lesser sounds ... then, suddenly, the gun-fire ceased and for a space we caught the fierce rattle of Mauser rifles followed by British infantry storming over the skyline, their bayonets flashing in the sun. Shouts and cries reached us, and we could see men desperately thrusting and clubbing. Then a rout of burghers broke back from the hill, streaming towards us in disorderly flight. The soldiers fired into them, bringing many down as they made blindly past us, not looking to right or left.

It was 27 February, the anniversary of Majuba. Buller, elated by the unusual taste of success, spent a good deal of the next day on Railway Hill watching the Boers retreating to the north-east. He made no attempt to harry the enemy further, and indeed an exceptionally violent storm on the night of the 27th had achieved as much as a massed cavalry charge might have done:

> The thunder was terrific, the rain was like an incessant water-spout, and the fearful lightning in its vivid play along the rocks and down the hill-sides revealed thousands of men bedraggled and drenched, rushing as fast as they could, no one seemed to know where. Some were on horseback, some in mule and bullock wagons, and many afoot, all hurrying on, along mountain-sides, over rushing rivers and sluits now turned into raging torrents; cattle and men, in some instances, being caught by the wild waters and hurled down by their fury to destruction; but on and on went the main body pell-mell, nobody apparently pursuing, only the frightful storm fiend and awful panic speeding them; and no human power could stay that rush on that memorable night.

Botha's force was broken. As they struggled to escape, the Afrikaners heard the news of Cronje's surrender at Paardeberg. They knew then that the siege of Ladysmith would have to be abandoned.

Within the Ladysmith defences Dr Kay chronicled these events:

27 February
News has arrived of the surrender of General Cronje after he lost 1,700 killed and wounded. Everyone very pleased. But the Boers in camp look miserable.

In the afternoon, after very heavy gunfire, we could hear Buller hard at it with rifle-firing; then as it began to get dusk it gradually slacked off.

28 February
Cloudy up to ten o'clock and not a shot to be heard, except one from Bulwana. About ten the sun came out and the helio was going gaily.

The Relief of Ladysmith: *Sir George White* 'I hoped to have met you before, Sir Redvers.'
132 *Sir Redvers Buller, VC,* 'Couldn't help it, General. Had so many Engagements.'

A few shots fired in the morning. At about three o'clock our 4·7 naval gun started blazing away at Bulwana. The opinion was that the guns were keeping the Boers from moving, and as we have not got much ammunition for the guns, we are sure we are near relief. But this morning we were put on half rations again.

Heavy rifle-fire was heard behind Bulwana about 4 p.m. At about 6 p.m. some mounted men were seen on the horizon going towards Caesar's Camp. Some said they were Boers, but as our guns did not open on them and as they were making towards Caesar's Camp, I felt sure they were part of Buller's forces.

Colonel Fawcett, 5th Lancers, who had a pair of field glasses, took a good look at them and said, 'Most decidedly they are British cavalry; the horses' tails are all cut short and it is relief at last.'

I don't know how others felt, speech was beyond me; and when we saw them turn towards Caesar's Camp, all knew his words were true. At last Ladysmith is relieved. Our 119 days of suffering are over, and with feelings impossible to describe I go to my tent and sit down alone. Thoughts of the past give way to hope for the future.

At home patriots exulted in the news that Ladysmith had been relieved. Enormous crowds rejoiced in the London streets, stopping the hansom cabs and delivery carts. Pall Mall blazed with torches, and art students from South Kensington marched to cheer Joseph Chamberlain.

In Ladysmith the citizens did not greet the relieving forces of Buller's army with wild enthusiasm. Hollow-eyed, and in their best clothes, they lined the streets and gave the soldiers a dutiful welcome. The war correspondent, J. B. Atkins, wrote ruefully, 'I have been greeted with as much ardour in an afternoon in London by a man with whom I had lunched two hours before.' Perhaps the garrison was too exhausted and listless to indulge in more dramatic displays. They had suffered considerable hardship, and few had enjoyed the lengthy game of waiting for Buller. Sir George White, however, put a much needed gloss on the whole affair in the brief speech he made as the long siege ended. 'I thank God,' he said, 'we have kept the flag flying.' It was just what the Empire wanted to hear.

Chapter 8

Marching to Pretoria

During the early days of March 1900 the Afrikaner leadership struggled desperately to halt the break-up of their forces and restore morale. It was no easy task. In north Natal the Boers flooded through Elandslaagte on their way home. Louis Botha and Lukas Meyer sought in vain for General Joubert, and threatened to shoot the horses of those who wanted to leave. But Elandslaagte, crammed with Boer supplies, had to be abandoned; rather than let its stores fall into British hands it was set on fire and the great column of smoke could be seen for fifty miles around.

It was small wonder that so many Boers shouted '*huis-toe*!' ('We're going home!') to their commanders, for their cause seemed lost. Kimberley and Ladysmith had been relieved; in the west an almost entire army had surrendered with Cronje; the offensive in north Natal had been broken, and invading columns ejected from the Cape Midlands; Lord Roberts stood at the head of a well equipped and confident army ready to advance on Bloemfontein. Nor was there any sign (or indeed practical possibility) of foreign intervention on their behalf. The British had now had a taste of victory and would undoubtedly drive home their advantages to the full.

President Kruger actively intervened to try to stop the Boers struggling into the most northerly reaches of Natal, to Glencoe and even Newcastle. By his entreaties and his exhortations Kruger managed to patch up the situation in north Natal, then he departed for Bloemfontein on 5 March leaving Joubert to cope with Boer strategy in that area.

At Bloemfontein, Kruger and President Steyn conferred; they made a peace proposal to the British government, but, since it stipulated the full independence of the two republics, it was hardly likely to be accepted. More significant was their determination to stand firm against Roberts's threatened advance from the west. They reckoned that, with reinforcements drawn from Natal, Colesburg and Stormberg, they could put twelve thousand men into the field against the invaders. Poplar Grove, set among a line of hills extending for twenty-five miles, and fifty miles from Bloemfontein, was chosen as the first line of defence; Christiaan de Wet was entrenched there with six thousand men.

Against this puny and over-extended force, Roberts could pit thirty thousand troops. On 7 March he resumed his march westwards. The line at Poplar Grove did not hold; the Boers did not wait to be enveloped by the infantry columns or encircled by French's cavalry; they outspanned their wagons and made off, President

Opposite Lord Kitchener (front, right) enters Johannesburg.

135

Kruger travelling with them in his Cape cart. French was particularly lethargic that day, nursing some petty grievances against Roberts, and making slow progress. If he had shown the dash that had relieved Kimberley and stopped Cronje in his tracks at Paardeberg, then another substantial Boer army might have been captured and President Kruger with it. Given such a catastrophe for the Afrikaners it is difficult to see how they could have persevered with the war.

As it was, Kruger was being carried along amid a panic-stricken mob. At Abram's Kraal, thirty-five miles from Bloemfontein, aided by de Wet and de la Rey, he managed partially to stop the rout, though units of the Zarps (the South African Republic's Police force) disobeyed his orders to shoot the fugitives. While Kruger and de Wet hastened back to Bloemfontein to organize its defences, de la Rey, with a mere fifteen hundred men (including a thousand Zarps), stayed at Abram's Kraal to resist Roberts.

On 10 March the British army, refurbished with fresh supplies, approached in three columns from the east. On the 11th, as Roberts rode out to join General French's cavalrymen at the front of the advance, he was troubled by rumours of heavy Boer reinforcements closing in from the north. Knowing how crucial it was to seize Bloemfontein, with its vital railway rolling stock, he decided to send French off to take Brand Kop four miles south-east of the city. Once this dominating hill was taken, Bloemfontein would be at the mercy of the British army.

At about 4 p.m. in the afternoon, French's weary horsemen cut the railway line out of Bloemfontein and approached Brand Kop as the daylight faded. Four hundred Boers were hustled off the ridge.

The capture of Brand Kop sealed the fate of Bloemfontein. The Afrikaners accepted the inevitability of its fall, and thousands of them trekked away to the north. President Steyn and his government left at night by train; the state archives had already been sent to Kroonstad a hundred miles away to the north.

On 13 March Lord Roberts was able to make his formal entry into Bloemfontein at the head of his cavalrymen. As he rode along the decorated streets, past pretty gardens and respectable buildings, the citizens gave him a warm reception. There were several reasons for this unexpected welcome: the hard-core resistance had left, to fight another day; there were a considerable number of British citizens in the city; moreover, the Orange Free State had traditionally enjoyed close economic links with the Cape, and hence with British power, thus the rock-solid basis of militant Afrikaner nationalism was not to be found in Bloemfontein.

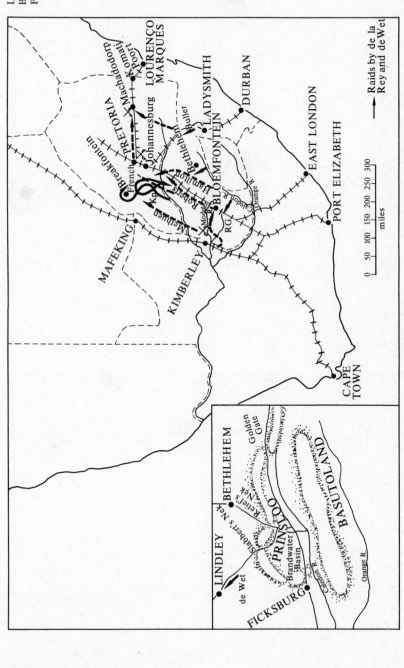

Lord Roberts' march to
Bloemfontein and
Pretoria.

LOURENÇO
MARQUES

Machadodorp
Komati
Poort
PRETORIA
Johannesburg
Breaktfontein
French
LADYSMITH
Bethlehem
Buller
DURBAN
Kroonstadt
Bethlehem
BLOEMFONTEIN
Roberts
Hamilton
EAST LONDON
Methuen
Modder R.
Orange R.
Caledon R.
R.G.
PORT ELIZABETH

MAFEKING

KIMBERLEY

→ Raids by de la
   Rey and de Wet

0 50 100 150 200 250 300
miles

CAPE
TOWN

LINDLEY
BETHLEHEM
de Wet
Golden
Gate
Relief's
Nek
Slabbert's Nek
PRINSLOO
Brandwater
Basin
Caledon R.
BASUTOLAND
Orange R.
FICKSBURG

137

With the occupation of Bloemfontein, Britain erupted with scenes of rejoicing. Both Houses of Parliament assembled in the courtyard of Buckingham Palace and serenaded Queen Victoria with a rendering of the National Anthem. The crowds in the streets were almost hysterical with joy, exulting in the turn of events that seemed to have brought the war close to its end. There was also a solid feeling of satisfaction that the continental critics of Britain would now have little to crow about. Yet the war was by no means universally popular; there were pro-Boers on the left wing of the Liberal party and among socialist groups, and both David Lloyd George and Keir Hardie advocated pro-Boer views, though they got rough receptions at public meetings; the Peace Society, and the League of Liberals Against Aggression and Militarism, made their voices heard. But the national mood was perhaps more accurately captured by *Punch* which showed a baby saying 'Bang!' as his first word.

In South Africa, while Roberts nursed his tired troops in preparation for the next big push, Kitchener busied himself with crushing rebellion in the western Cape, and other British columns brought much of the southern Orange Free State under imperial control. More than eight thousand Free Staters and Cape rebels laid down their arms, though the ultimate fate of the latter (pardon or punishment) was left to the British authorities to decide. At Bloemfontein, Roberts's main task was to restore the railway system necessary for the supplies that were so vital to his future progress, and to make proper use of the 200,000 men now in South Africa.

The Afrikaner leaders tried to cope with the gloom that had seized so many of their supporters. In Pretoria, President Kruger was confronted by a legal deputation, led by Chief Justice Gregorowski, which urged him, unsuccessfully, to call a halt to the war. President Steyn, ousted from his capital, physically imposing, cultured and intelligent, did his utmost to restore morale. On 27 March Commandant-General Piet Joubert died, and Louis Botha took his place. This promotion led to a greater drive for efficiency among the remaining Boer forces, of which there were about 12,500 near Bloemfontein and 15,500 on other fronts. It was agreed, for example, that military courts should impose sterner discipline, and that the regulations for leave should be tightened up. It was also resolved that generals should have the power to limit the number of transport wagons under their command; this was meant to reduce the numbers of wives and children attached to the Afrikaner columns, an encumbrance which had, arguably, brought Cronje to disaster at Paardeberg. Not all Boers accepted these new regulations, and de Wet, for instance, had to force Commandant Vilonel of

Opposite S. Begg's 'Sons of the Blood'. A patriotic excess, appropriate for the times.

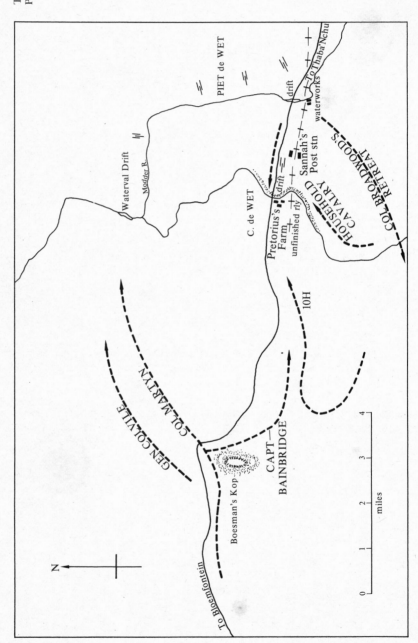

The Battle of Sannah's
Post, 31 March 1900.

140

Winberg to resign because he refused to abide by the decision of the Council of War regarding excess wagons.

It was de Wet, in fact, with his brother Piet, who gave the British at Bloemfontein the most trouble. He decided to move down from the north and attack the waterworks on the Modder upon which Bloemfontein largely depended. This resulted in the Battle of Sannah's Post (named after the railway station on the unfinished line to the east).

De Wet's tactics were simple. His brother Piet was to lead the larger part of his force of two thousand men in an attack upon the waterworks from the east bank of the Modder; meanwhile he would wait on the west side of the river and destroy the small British force guarding the waterworks (two hundred men) as they were driven towards him. De Wet did not envisage interference from other British troops. There were some British twelve miles away at Springfield, a few at Boesman's Kop (about eight miles from the waterworks), also a convoy of wagons, escorted by cavalry under Colonel Broadwood, somewhere to the east of the Modder, but de Wet fancied that they might run up against Commandant Oliver and several thousand Boers, who were in that area.

An hour before dawn on the day de Wet had picked for his attack, some of his men discovered that a column of carts carrying English-speaking refugees was starting to cross the river from the east. He described the scene in his book *Three Years' War*:

> As soon as it became light enough to see anything we discovered that just above the spruit stood a wagon with some Kaffirs and a number of sheep and cattle beside it. The Kaffirs told us that the wagon belonged to one of the 'hands-uppers' [Boers who co-operated with the British] from Thaba 'Nchu, and that they had been ordered to get it down to Bloemfontein as quickly as possible and sell it to the English. The owner of the sheep and of the cattle, they said, was with General Broadwood whose troops had just arrived at the waterworks. The light grew brighter and there, three thousand paces from us, was Broadwood's huge force.

De Wet quickly saw that he had almost stumbled into a trap himself. A large force of cavalry (in all, about two thousand men) was bivouacked around the waterworks. De Wet decided, however, that he could deal with this force by the same tactics as he had prepared for the small one. Anxiously he waited for the sound of his brother's guns opening fire. He did not have long to wait:

> Then our guns began to fire; and the result was a scene of confusion. Towards us over the brow of the hill came the wagons pell-mell, with a   141

few carts moving rapidly to the front. When the first of these reached the spruit its occupants – a man and a woman beside him – became aware that something was wrong. I was standing at the top of the drift with Commandants Fourie and Nel. I immediately ordered two of my adjutants to mount the cart and sit at the driver's side. The other carts came one after another into the drift, and I ordered them to follow close behind the first cart, at the same time warning the occupants that if they gave any signal to the enemy they would be shot. The carts were filled with English from Thaba 'Nchu. I was very glad that the women and children should reach a place of safety before the fighting began. So speedily did the carts follow each other that the English had no suspicion of what was occurring, and very shortly the soldiers began to pour into the drift in the greatest disorder. As soon as they reached the stream, they were met by the cry of 'Hands up!' Directly they heard the words a forest of hands rose in the air. More troops quickly followed, and we had disarmed two hundred before they had time to know what was happening.

De Wet might well have captured more of the British troops, but for a couple of artillery officers who came down to the drift across the river imagining that there was some sort of transport tangle to sort out. Both officers were surprised to encounter de Wet, who said quietly, 'Dismount. You are prisoners. Go to the wagons.' The leading battery came on, and was also captured. Suddenly one of the captured officers decided to run for it; he broke away, yelling a warning to the second battery, that was now approaching the drift. The battery (Q Battery) immediately wheeled round, and galloped off.

At this point, de Wet and his men opened fire on them. Q Battery in fact halted a little further off, and, joined by an escaped gun team from the drift, began to bombard de Wet's positions, but to little effect. Colonel Broadwood's men were now uncomfortably caught between the fire of both the de Wets' forces, and a small British force that had arrived at Boesman's Kop was split in two and thus of little real help.

At 10 a.m. Broadwood decided to rescue the guns of Q Battery, and to try to escape to the south-west. There now followed an episode that was much cherished by patriots at home: volunteers ran out to drag off the threatened guns and limbers, though subjected to merciless rifle fire; four VCs were won, and when the attempt was at last called off the watching British troops rose to cheer the gallant rescuers.

Eventually Broadwood made his escape, but de Wet had won the day. The British lost six hundred men, eighty out of ninety wagons, and seven of the twelve guns; Bloemfontein's water supply

was cut off, and within a month two thousand inhabitants had died of enteric fever. De Wet crowned his triumph at Sannah's Post by next day swooping down on four hundred of General Gatacre's troops at Mostert's Hoek; by the time Gatacre himself arrived on the scene he found that his men had tamely surrendered and been taken off.

Military cemetery at Bloemfontein.

Neither this episode nor the disaster at Sannah's Post boded well for Britain's hope of finishing off Boer resistance quickly. De Wet's mobility and incisiveness showed what success even small numbers of determined men could achieve; moreover, he had been aided in his coup at Mostert's Hoek by burghers who had been prepared to break their recently taken oath of non-participation in the fighting.

Still, by now, the beginning of April 1900, Lord Roberts was ready to lead his army out of Bloemfontein. Roberts was determined to march straight for the Transvaal's capital of Pretoria, believing that its capture would effectively end the war, not merely because of the effect of its fall upon Boer morale, but also because it was the railway centre for all the main lines except the Western Railway. En route he would enter Johannesburg, the golden city, citadel of the Uitlanders, and the source of so much of the wealth of Kruger's republic.

It seemed unlikely that the Boers could stop the British march on Pretoria. Roberts had over 170,000 men in the field, and proposed to use 100,000 of them in his great northwards advance; the rest were to be left behind in garrisons, or to guard the vitally important supply and communications lines for the main army. The Afrikaners had about thirty thousand fighting men, mostly in small forces

143

scattered over a large area.

Roberts proposed to head the main advance himself: three columns, totalling 38,000 troops, with over 100 guns. Meanwhile, to the west of the north-south railway line, Lord Methuen would also march towards the Transvaal. The eastern flank of the British advance was vulnerable, however. At first Roberts tried to persuade Buller, in north Natal, to swing his army across in support. But, as usual, Buller prevaricated, piling excuse upon excuse: he had, he said, insufficient cavalry, infantry, engineers, equipment, boots, clothes, (but not food). Roberts finally gave up trying to pin him down to a definite plan of campaign and left him to make his own way, at his own speed, into the Transvaal.

While Roberts was laying his plans, Mafeking was still under siege. Baden-Powell had let his Commander-in-Chief know that the town's supplies would be finished by 22 May. Roberts therefore ordered a flying column to be detached from the forces stationed at Kimberley to go to the relief of Mafeking.

At 5 a.m. on 3 May, Roberts took the train from Bloemfontein. Alighting at Karee Siding he placed himself at the head of the column that he was confident he would soon be leading into Pretoria. This column included units representing all those countries of the Empire that had sent troops to support the British cause in South Africa. As the infantry stepped it out, spirits were high, and on all sides men were singing 'We are marching to Pretoria!' The refrain had an ominous ring for the waiting Afrikaners.

Those Boers that waited to try to stem the tide of the British advance had an almost impossible task. De la Rey's men were appalled at the sight of tens of thousands of enemy troops spilling towards them over open ground; they retreated smartly from Brandfort (fifteen miles from Bloemfontein), and made a brief stand at the Vet River on 5 May.

At Kroonstad, his temporary capital, President Steyn, with Louis Botha and about eight thousand men to support him, struggled to inspire his people's will to resist:

Look, burghers! There are your brothers [men on a train drawing out of Kroonstad for the front] going forward to take part in the struggle which you and I have to carry on to its end; and are you going to stand here while they are fighting for their country? ... We have fought against the hordes of Great Britain for more than seven months; we can fight seven times as long if necessary. Go, then, burghers, in God's name, for the cause of your dear country, for your wives and children. It is better to die on the battlefield than to become slaves of your ancient enemy.

But the Boers could not stand at Sand River: the British columns threatened to envelop them, and their only alternative to encirclement was flight. Steyn saw the realities too, and on 11 May he declared Heilbron, sixty miles to the north-east, to be his new capital. On 12 May Roberts marched into Kroonstad; there was no resistance.

As Roberts's men swarmed northwards, the Transvaal's parliament (the Volksraad) met. With the news that more British reinforcements, and heavy siege guns, had recently arrived in South Africa, the Volksraad decided that Pretoria could not be properly defended; it was agreed, therefore, to fight the British before they reached the Transvaal's capital. As they dispersed, many delegates must have been privately convinced that they would never again assemble under an independent republican constitution.

While the British were occupying Kroonstad, the flying column under Colonel Mahon was approaching Mafeking. Even as the British drew near, a determined group of Boers led by Field-Cornet Sarel Eloff, a grandson of Paul Kruger, broke through Mafeking's outer defences on 12 May 1900. Baden-Powell drummed up all available troops and soon forced Eloff to surrender, at the same time personally inviting him to dinner.

The next day, 13 May, Mahon's column joined up with Colonel Plumer who had marched to the Molopo twenty miles from Mafeking. On 16 May the combined British forces drove several thousand Boers off the Molopo River at a place called Israel's Farm. This was the effective end of the siege of Mafeking. At 7 p.m. on 17 May ten troopers of the Imperial Light Horse, led by Major Karri Davis, rode into Mafeking.

On 18 May at about 9.30 p.m. a Reuter message told London that Mafeking had been relieved. Soon the Mansion House dangled a placard from a window, announcing the good tidings. As the news spread like a forest fire throughout the capital, theatre performances were interrupted, and huge crowds whirled into the streets, cheering, dancing and singing patriotic songs. But it was not merely London that was caught up in the tumultuous celebrations:

> Liverpool was alive with parading crowds; Newcastle was startled by the explosion and flare of rockets; Birmingham spread the news like wildfire from its theatres; the brass band of the volunteers roused the streets of York; Glasgow illuminated its Municipal Buildings; Leicester and Brighton swarmed with madly cheering people; the Yorkshire dales reverberated with the sound of strangely blown mill and factory sirens.

The next day was Saturday, a half-holiday for many people anyway. The pandemonium continued unabated; red, white and blue bunting was everywhere; London's main streets were clogged with revellers, and street-hawkers (and pick-pockets) did a roaring trade. As evening fell, bonfires were lit; there was singing and dancing in the street. There was also a good deal of drunkenness and hooliganism, and one policeman who had been deluged with kisses at Aldgate said plainly, 'I wouldn't go through that kissing again for anything. Right in the public street it was.'

The Mafeking celebrations added a verb, to 'maffick', to the language; they disgusted opponents of the war, and even gave pause to serious-minded supporters of imperial expansion; they were both vulgar and fun, distressing and exhilarating. Essentially the pandemonium was pathetic, the relieved reaction of a nation fed on grandiose notions of imperial might, but, underneath all the glitter, pomp and circumstance, insecure, resentful of international hostility, and embarrassed at the war's early fiascos. Posterity may be forgiven, indeed, for asking what all the fuss was about.

Lord Roberts's army rested at Kroonstad for ten days. Then, on 22 May, it struck off northwards again, for Johannesburg and Pretoria. British forces were pressing on the Transvaal from all sides, and there was little active opposition to their advance.

On 24 May French's cavalry reached the Vaal River; on the same day Roberts announced the annexation of the Orange Free State. Inexorably the march on Johannesburg continued. Louis Botha fell back before it, his numbers dwindling as the British came on. At last, he and three thousand men stood barring Roberts's way at Klip River a few miles south of Johannesburg. Here Botha, supported by Koos de la Rey, newly arrived from Mafeking, managed to hold up the British advance for the best part of two days. But the enemy's numbers, and French's swooping raids, proved too much; the Boers found themselves outflanked, and retreated.

Roberts marched into Johannesburg on 31 May 1900, and a silken Union Jack, made by his wife, was hoisted at the courthouse. Most of the Uitlanders, for whom, in theory, the war was being fought, had left, and Johannesburg was something of a ghost town as a result. In nearby Pretoria, Paul Kruger prepared to move sixty miles down the Delagoa Bay railway to Middleburg. In Britain, the fall of Johannesburg aroused little enthusiasm – certainly nothing like the reaction to the news of Paardeberg or of the relief of the besieged towns. On the stock exchange, however, there was gratification that, contrary to earlier threats, the Boers had not 146 blown up the gold mines and valuable industrial equipment.

On 3 June Roberts was poised for the climax of his three hundred-mile march to Pretoria. With General French riding ahead with orders to sweep round Pretoria from the west and to cut the central railway line north of the city, the British columns moved off over rolling, brown hill country; they had forty miles to go.

In Pretoria panic had gripped much of the populace. Government stores were looted, and there was a mass exodus in whatever trains were still running (to the east), in carts and wagons, or on foot, pushing wheelbarrows and hand-carts laden with private possessions. Kruger left his capital, and entrained for Machadodorp which was destined to be his seat of government until he was forced to flee the country in September; Schalk Burger, the Vice-President, stayed on in Pretoria; so, for a while, did the State-Attorney Jan Smuts – soon to go into the field as a commando leader. The courageous and unfortunate Botha was entrusted with the defence of Pretoria, which was a thankless task, since he had barely two thousand men, and the city's modern forts had been stripped of guns in the earlier part of the war.

Lord Roberts at the head of a column of men in South Africa.

147

Botha, ever a realist, proposed that the Transvaal should now surrender, but de la Rey swore that he would never accept this and would continue to fight on in the east. Botha decided, however, that Pretoria was indefensible, and he abandoned the city and withdrew whatever loyal troops he had eastwards.

Lord Roberts, with Lord Kitchener at his side, arrived at Pretoria's central square at 2.15 p.m. on 5 June. At the government buildings the Union Jack, that had been hauled down after Majuba, was reinstated amid thunderous cheers. A victory march past followed, 'Bobs' savouring the triumphant climax to his epic advance from Bloemfontein. He had made the three hundred-mile march in thirty-four days, the vast bulk of his army slogging away on foot, carrying all their food and supplies with them. His foes had been scattered like chaff before him. The war seemed well and truly won.

Of course there was still some mopping up to be done. On 7 June, moreover, de Wet overran some garrisons along the railway line north of Kroonstad, causing the British over seven hundred losses. While Kitchener was sent south to restore the severed communication links, Roberts turned against Botha's remaining forces astride the railway line to Mozambique at Diamond Hill, twenty-five miles east of Pretoria. With considerable difficulty the British troops managed to occupy part of Diamond Hill by nightfall on 11 June. But the next morning, when the offensive was renewed, it was discovered that the Boers had slipped away under cover of darkness, and had made off down the railway line towards Kruger at Machadodorp. The Battle of Diamond Hill was one of the last formal, face-to-face encounters of the war.

One more significant operation came in July 1900, when the British tried to break continuing Boer resistance in the north-east of the Orange Free State. South of Bethlehem about nine thousand Afrikaners were hemmed in the Brandwater Basin by sixteen thousand British troops. Among the Boers were President Steyn, who had been harried from one makeshift capital to another, and Commandants de Wet and Prinsloo. In desperation the trapped Boers decided to try to break out through the few as yet unguarded passes. Four columns were formed, but only the one under de Wet and President Steyn managed to escape. The others were less fortunate and over four thousand men under Prinsloo, with four thousand sheep and six thousand horses, were eventually forced to surrender. De Wet, whose escape was to cause the British untold tribulation later in the year, afterwards wrote scathingly of these events:

> On 17 and 18 July the enemy had broken through at Slabbert's Nek and Retief's Nek, causing the greatest confusion among our forces. Many of the officers and burghers were for an immediate surrender, as appears from the fact that the same assembly which, in defiance of law, elected Mr Prinsloo as Commander-in-Chief, also decided by seventeen votes to thirteen, to give up their forces to the enemy. But this decision was at once rescinded, and it was agreed to ask for an armistice of six days to enable them to take counsel with the Government. A more senseless course of action could hardly be imagined. The Boer Army, as anyone could see, was in a very tight place. Did its officers think that the English would be so foolish as to grant an armistice at such a time as this when all the burghers wanted was a few days in which to effect their escape? Either the officers were remarkably short-sighted or ... something worse. It was still possible for the commanders to retire in the direction of Witzieshock (through Golden Gate). But instead of getting this done with all speed, Mr Prinsloo began a correspondence with General Hunter about this ridiculous armistice, which the English of course refused to grant. On 29 July 1900 Prinsloo, with all the burghers on the mountains, surrendered unconditionally to the enemy. What then is to be our judgment on this act of Prinsloo and the other chief officers there? That it was nothing short of an act of murder, committed on the Government, the country and the Nation, to surrender three thousand men [sic] in such a way. Even the burghers themselves cannot be held to have been altogether without guilt, though they can justly plead that they were obeying orders. The sequel of Prinsloo's surrender was on a par with it. A large number of burghers from Harrismith and a small part of Vrede commando, although they had already made good their escape, rode quietly from their farms into Harrismith and there surrendered to General Sir Hector Macdonald – one could gnash one's teeth to think that a nation should so readily rush to its own ruin!

149

Lord Roberts' bilingual announcement of the resignation of President Kruger.

In August, while Roberts was concentrating on linking up with Buller (at last) and scouring the north-east Transvaal of the enemy, de Wet, de la Rey and others were making a nuisance of themselves south and west of Pretoria. Though the British managed to scatter Botha's forces once more, near Belfast, after an heroic resistance by the Zarps, it was the commandos' operations in the west that had greater portent. Unless the British could promptly round up the widely separated groups of Boers that were still fighting, there seemed no end to the havoc they could create by attacking lines of communications, garrisons, store depôts and the like.

For President Kruger, though, the war had ended. On 11 September he entrained for Delagoa Bay, and thence sailed for Holland. Few imagined that he would return. He had, as a boy, taken part in the Great Trek, he now saw, as an old man, his republic smashed to pieces by the British army. In fact, with the annexation of the Transvaal, both Afrikaner states had ceased to exist, and at Cape Town Sir Alfred Milner would soon be chafing to 'suspend' the Cape constitution and forcibly federate all of South Africa.

In Britain, the Unionist government sought to cash in on the apparent victory in South Africa by appealing to the electorate for a renewed mandate. The 'Khaki Election' of October 1900 was bitterly contested, particularly by those who hated 'Chamberlain's War'. The results confirmed the Unionists in office with a slightly enlarged majority; although this could be interpreted as a mandate for pushing the war through to the bitter end, it did not escape notice that for every eight votes cast for the government seven were cast against it.

In the same month General Buller departed for home, leaving the care of his soldiers' stomachs to others. At the end of November, Lord Roberts laid down his command and returned to a triumphant and rapturous reception in Britain. Queen Victoria bestowed an earldom upon him and also made him a Knight of the Garter; Parliament voted him £100,000, and everywhere he was fêted and admired. In fact, the celebrations were sadly premature. The commandos in the field did not lay down their arms; the fall of Bloemfontein and Pretoria, even the flight of Kruger, did not bring about the pacification of South Africa. The war still had one and a half years to run.

Chapter 9

Kitchener in Command

While the British public was according Lord Roberts a reception suitable for a conquering hero, Kitchener of Khartoum was grappling with the realities of the situation in South Africa. Having annexed the Boer republics the British government was now demanding unconditional surrender from the Afrikaner forces that were still at large. But unconditional surrender could only come if the commandos were decisively beaten in the field, or trapped, by the overwhelmingly large British army in South Africa.

The fall of Bloemfontein and Pretoria, the defeat and capture of Cronje's army at Paardeberg, the flight of President Kruger, and the discomfiture of President Steyn, though serious blows to the Afrikaner cause did not in themselves force capitulation upon those Boers who were still prepared to fight. Just as Napoleon had fought his way to Moscow in 1812 and had then found no government with which to negotiate a peace settlement, so the British discovered that their triumphs did not lead directly to the conference table.

In all the Commando War effectively lasted from March 1900 to 31 May 1902 when the war ended. The commandos had a huge area in which to continue their resistance. There were railway lines to cut, garrisons to surprise, supply columns to ambush. Given skilful leadership, the Boer forces would be extraordinarily difficult to run to earth. They would, moreover, be sustained and aided by the Afrikaner civilian population. It should not be supposed that the Boers hoped to defeat their enemies, but, if they could protract the war, they might force Britain to negotiate a reasonable peace settlement; or a Liberal government might succeed the Unionists and be more inclined to treat the defeated republics gently.

The spirit of Boer resistance was best exemplified by Christiaan de Wet. Elusive, wily, brave and imaginative, de Wet's exploits thrilled not only his own people but also a substantial section of the British public – which accorded him a hero's welcome when he came to London, with Botha and de la Rey, to negotiate with the British government in August 1902.

In December 1900 it looked as if de Wet would be caught in a trap sprung by Kitchener as he tried to cross the Orange River to raid Cape Colony:

> That evening we reached the Orange River; but alas! what a sight met our eyes! The river was quite impassable owing to the floods, and, in addition, the ford was held by English troops stationed on the south bank. Our position was beginning to be critical, for there were English garrisons guarding the bridges and fords of the Orange on our south,

and those of the Caledon on our north. There was still Basutoland [north-east between the rivers] but we did not wish to cross its borders – we were on good terms with the Basutos and we could not afford to make enemies of them. Surely we had enough enemies already! The reader will now perceive how it was my projected inroad into Cape Colony did not become a fact. My dear old friend, General Charles Knox [in charge of the British columns], was against it, and he had the best of the argument for the river was unfordable. What then was I to do? Retreat I could not, for the Caledon was also now full. Again, as I have already explained, it would not do for me to take refuge in Basutoland ... I knew that the Orange and Caledon Rivers sometimes remained unfordable for weeks together. How could I escape then? Oh, the English had caught me at last! They hemmed me in on every side; I could not get away from them. In fact they had 'cornered me', to use one of their own favourite expressions. That they also thought so appears from what I read afterwards in the *South African News* where I saw that Lord Kitchener had given orders to General Charles Knox 'not to take prisoners there'! For the truth of this I cannot positively vouch; but it was a very suspicious circumstance that the editor of the newspaper was afterwards thrown into prison for having published this very anecdote about Lord Kitchener ...

Without delay I proceeded to the Commissiedrift bridge over the Caledon. As I feared it was occupied by the enemy [Highland Light Infantry]. Entrenchments had been dug, and schanzes thrown up at both ends. Foiled here, I at once sent a man to see if the river was still rising. It might be the case that there had not been so much rain higher up. The man reported that the river was falling, and would be fordable [upstream] by the evening. This was good news indeed ... Accordingly we made for Sevenfontein, a ford ten or twelve miles further up the river. If it were not already in the enemy's hands, we would surely be able to get across there. Shortly before sunset we arrived at Sevenfontein. To our immense joy, it was unoccupied and fordable.

De Wet made his way north towards Dewetsdorp (named after an ancestor) and Thaba 'Nchu. Once more British forces closed in on him; General Knox's men standing before him, and other columns pressing in. But General Piet Fourie, who was with de Wet, saw a gap in the British line and, despite fierce fire from either side, the Boers burst through. De Wet later described this narrow escape:

On either side of the way we passed, there were two strong forts (schanzes), at a distance of from a thousand to twelve hundred paces from each other. In the space between them was absolutely no cover; and the distance from the point where the burghers were first visible to the men in these forts, to the point where they again disappeared from view was at least three thousand paces. Over these terrible three thousand paces our burghers raced, while a storm of bullets was poured in upon them from both sides. And of all that force – eight thousand strong – no single man was killed, and only one was wounded! Our

Blockhouses and fences constructed by the end of the war; also Jan Smuts' invasion of Cape Colony from June 1901 to May 1902.

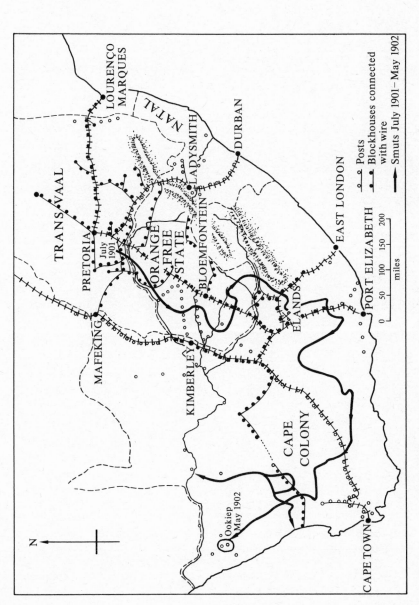

○ ─ ○ Posts
● ─ ● Blockhouses connected with wire
━━━ Smuts July 1901– May 1902

TRANSVAAL

LOURENÇO MARQUES

NATAL

PRETORIA

July 1901

ORANGE FREE STATE

LADYSMITH

DURBAN

BLOEMFONTEIN

MAFEKING

KIMBERLEY

ELANDS

EAST LONDON

PORT ELIZABETH

CAPE COLONY

Ookiep May 1902

CAPE TOWN

N

0   50   100 150 200
miles

155

The elusive Christiaan de Wet (third from the right) and his staff.

marvellous escape can only be described to the providence and irresistible protection of Almighty God, who kept His hand graciously over us. What the enemy's loss was I never heard. In addition to the burghers, a few carts and wagons, and one gun got safely through the English lines.

So de Wet had escaped again. Whether or not this was due to the intervention of the Almighty, Kitchener, by the beginning of 1901, had come to the conclusion that a massive series of barbed wire fences must be built across the veld; at intervals there should be blockhouses, encased with two layers of corrugated iron packed with stones. At first the wire barriers and blockhouses were widely separated from each other, but gradually the British closed the distances by building more fences. Some commandos were indeed trapped by this system. De Wet, however, was more elusive, and later wrote, in somewhat dismissive tones:

> I learnt that the enemy were occupied in building a line of blockhouses from Heilbron to Frankfort [N.E. of Orange Free State]. It had always seemed to me a most unaccountable circumstance that England – the all-powerful – could not catch the Boers without the aid of these blockhouses ... Still, narrower and narrower did the circle become, hemming us in more closely at every moment. The result was that they 'bagged' an

enormous number of men and cattle, without a solitary burgher or, for the matter of that, a solitary ox, having been captured by means of their famous blockhouse system. The English have been constantly boasting in the newspapers about the advantages of their blockhouses; but they have never been able to give an instance of a capture effected by them. On the contrary, when during the later stages of the war, it happened, as it often did, that they drove some of our men against one or other of the great blockhouse lines which then intersected the country, and it became necessary for us to fight our way through, we generally succeeded in doing so … There were thousands of miles of blockhouse lines which made a sort of spider's web of the South African Republics. The blockhouses themselves were sometimes round, sometimes angled erections. The roofs were always of iron. The walls were pierced with loop-holes four feet from the ground, and from four to six feet from each other. Between the blockhouses were fences, made with five strands of barbed-wire. Parallel with these was a trench, three feet deep and four to five feet across the top, but narrower at the bottom. Where the material could be procured, there was also a stone wall to serve as an additional obstacle. Sometimes there were two lines of fences, the upper one – erected on top of the earth thrown up from the trench – consisting of three or four strands only. There was thus a regular network of wires in the vicinity of the blockhouses – the English seemed to think that a Boer might be netted like a fish.

Still, the blockhouse system undeniably put great pressure upon de Wet and others. So did the attempt by the British to keep a watch on the drifts over the rivers. De Wet described yet another narrow escape as he approached the Vaal River near the appropriately named Bothaville in the north-west of the Orange Free State:

On the night of 12 March we broke through the blockhouse line, some five miles to the west of Bothaville. When we were about fifty paces from the line, somebody to our left challenged us:

'Halt! Who goes there?'

He challenged us a second time, and then fired. At once seven or eight sentries fired upon us. Shots also were directed at us from the right. Nevertheless we cut through the barbed-wire and crossed in safety, the firing still continuing until we were about fifteen hundred paces on the far side of the line. Fortunately no one was hit. Having thus escaped the last 'White Elephant' that we should have to reckon with, the next obstacle to be encountered was the Vaal River. For President Steyn [who was in the field with de Wet] … had decided to visit de la Rey in order to place himself under medical advice. His eyes had become very weak during the last fortnight or so, and he thought that Dr van Rennenkampf might be able to do something for them. Thus we had to cross the Vaal River.

But we heard that there was a military post at Commando Drift where we wanted to cross, and further, that all the other fords were occupied by the English. We should have been in a great difficulty had not one of our burghers, Pieterson, who knew the district thoroughly,   157

Farm-burning was part of the British campaign to deny the Boer forces adequate supplies.

Farm-burning was part of the British campaign to deny the Boer forces adequate supplies.

brought us across the river by a footpath ford. We crossed on 15 March. The current was so strong that in places the river-bed was strewn with huge boulders, over which our steeds had to climb. However we all managed to get safely over ... on the following day we joined General de la Rey.

De Wet's exploits made him a household name throughout the world. In Britain, where his elusiveness was the despair of patriots and a consolation to pro-Boers, he became a legend. King Edward VII once said jocularly of a hostess bent on finding a suitor for her daughter that 'they ought to set her to catch de Wet'. Rudyard Kipling, bard of Empire and a journalist in South Africa during the war, wrote wryly in his poem dedicated to the Royal Artillery and entitled 'Ubique':

Ubique means 'They've caught de Wet, an' now we shan't be long.'
Ubique means 'I much regret, the beggar's goin' strong!'

To help the British army track down commando leaders like de Wet, and to punish those who aided them, Lord Roberts had begun a policy of farm-burning in the Orange Free State in June 1900. Technically those Free Staters who aided Boer forces were rebels, since the republic had been annexed by the British crown in May, and between June and November 1900 more than six hundred farms were burnt. Farm-burning was also practised in the Transvaal,

158

and actively prosecuted by Kitchener in his attempts to smash Afrikaner resistance. It was a policy which aroused bitter resentment among the Afrikaners and mixed feeling among the British troops that actually set fire to the homesteads.

Captain R. F. Talbot of the Royal Horse Artillery wrote in his diary for 1901:

> I went out this morning with some of my men ostensibly to get vegetables, but joined the provost marshal and the sappers in a farm-burning party, and we burnt and blew up two farms with gun-cotton, turning out the inhabitants first. It is a bit sickening at first burning out the women and children, but they are such brutes and the former all spies; we don't mind it now. Only those are done which belong to men who are sniping or otherwise behaving badly.

Captain Phillipps, of 'Rimington's Guides', gave another, more poignant account of farm-burning in his book *With Rimington* published in 1902:

> I had to go myself the other day, at the General's bidding, to burn a farm near the line of march. We got to the place and I gave the inmates, three women and some children, ten minutes to clear their clothes and things out of the house, and my men then fetched bundles of straw and we proceeded to burn it down. The old grandmother was very angry. She told me that, though I was making a fine blaze now, it was nothing compared to the flames that I myself should be consumed in hereafter. Most of them however, were too miserable to curse. The women cried and the children stood by holding on to them and looking with large frightened eyes at the burning house. They won't forget that sight. I'll bet a sovereign, not even when they grow up. We rode away and left them, a forlorn little group, standing among their household goods – beds, furniture, and gimcracks strewn about the veldt; the crackling of the fire in their ears, and smoke and flame streaming overhead. The worst moment is when you first come to the house. The people thought we had called for refreshments, and one of the women went to get milk. Then we had to tell them that we had come to burn the place down. I simply didn't know which way to look. One of the women's husbands had been killed at Magersfontein. There were others, men and boys, away fighting; whether dead or alive they did not know ...
>
> We can't exterminate the Dutch or seriously reduce their numbers. We can do enough to make hatred of England and thirst for revenge the first duty of every Dutchman, and we can't effectively reduce the numbers of the men who will carry that duty out. Of course it is not a question of the war only. It is a question of governing the country afterwards.
>
> So far we only really hold the ground on which our armies stand. If I were to walk out from this tent a mile or two over the hills yonder, I should probably be shot. Kroonstad has been ours for four months. It is on the main railway. The country all round is being repeatedly crossed

by our troops. Yet an Englishman would not be safe for a minute out of range of those guns on the hill ...

At another farm a small girl interrupted her preparation for departure to play indignantly their National Anthem at us on an old piano. We were carting the people off. It was raining hard and blowing – a miserable, hurried home-leaving; ransacked house, muddy soldiers, a distracted mother saving one or two trifles and pushing along her children to the ox-wagon outside, and this poor little wretch in the midst of it all pulling herself together to strum a final defiance. One smiled, but it was rather dramatic all the same, and exactly like a picture.

Farm-burning was, in the short term, of some benefit to the British army. De Wet admitted as much when he wrote:

I had to wait there [near Heilbron] till the evening of 31 December until the necessary wagons and oxen had been got together for carrying the ammunition with us. Wagons were now no longer easily to be got, because the British had not only taken them away from the farms but had also burnt many of them ... even where there were wagons the women had always to keep them in readiness to fly in them before the columns of the enemy, who had now already command to carry the women away from their dwellings to the concentration camps – which the British called Refugee Camps. Proclamations had been issued by Lord Roberts, prescribing that any building within ten miles of the railway, where the Boers had blown up the railway line, should be burnt down.

160   In the long term, however, farm-burning antagonized many South

African moderates, and made the policy of postwar reconstruction more difficult, and much more expensive. Three Cape Colony editors were put on trial for criticizing this, and other aspects of British military policy, and in the fallen Afrikaner republics enraged villagers often refused to allow British dead to be buried in their cemeteries.

But the outraged reaction to farm-burning was overshadowed by the concentration camp controversy. The camps were first established in the summer of 1900, chiefly to protect the Hensoppers ('hands-uppers') from the vengeance of their fellow Afrikaners. As the war progressed, however, the families of prisoners of war (who were themselves mostly sent to Ceylon, Bermuda and St Helena), of men still fighting, or simply of those whose farms had been burnt, were placed in the camps.

There was, it must be assumed, no malevolent motive in the establishment of the concentration camps, despite the latter-day emotive connotations of the term. The camps were set up mostly in the Free State and the Transvaal, though there was also a number in the Cape and Natal. At one time they contained as many as 160,000 inmates. A direct result of the British occupation of the Boer republics and of the scorched earth aftermath of that success, they were simply a pragmatic response to certain problems.

But by October 1901 the concentration camps had acquired a terrible notoriety. Overcrowding, insanitary conditions, an insufficiently balanced diet and inadequate planning caused a tragic loss of life. Women and children, swept into the camps from isolated farms, were an easy prey to epidemic diseases, and measles, typhoid, jaundice, malaria, bronchitis and pneumonia all took their toll. In October 1901 there were as many as 3,156 deaths, and the annual average was running at 344 per thousand.

Not only did the death rate in the concentration camps convince many Afrikaners that the British were bent on destroying their race, but it led to a persistent and noisy outcry in the United Kingdom. The Liberal leader of the opposition, Sir Henry Campbell-Bannerman, felt moved to ask 'When is a war not a war? When it is carried on by methods of barbarism in South Africa.' 'Methods of barbarism' was a phrase which highlighted a memorable controversy. But the actual improvement in conditions in the camps owed much to the persistent agitation of Emily Hobhouse, Secretary of the Women's Branch of the South African Conciliation Committee ('that bloody woman', as Kitchener described her). As a result, conditions were drastically improved, and by the end of the war the death rate was down to sixty-nine per thousand.

The redoubtable Emily Hobhouse, Secretary of the Women's Branch of the South African
162   Conciliation Committee.

Despite the liberal and humanitarian outcry, there were plenty to defend the camps. Dr Alec Kay, safely out of Ladysmith, wrote scathingly of the 'agitation ... raised by a few unsexed and hysterical women who are prepared to sacrifice everything for notoriety'. He went on, writing in 1901:

The whole question of the camps is bound up with that of guerilla warfare. If it is lawful and necessary to destroy such Boer houses and farms that are used as bases for warfare is it not more humane to establish camps where women and children can be housed? And even at those Boer farms which have not been destroyed, the exigencies of war have brought a desperate shortage of food and medical attention and a constant danger from marauding natives against unarmed women and children. Is it not better for them to be taken to camps than be left where they are? All the misery, the burning and the camps are the result of war; it has always happened, and will happen again. After all it was the Boer Government which declared war.

It is true that there has been sickness in the camps and that conditions have been primitive. But they were set up hurriedly by the military authorities, and there is always disorganisation and lack of careful planning where large numbers of people are moved. Improvements are taking place rapidly, and they would have taken place whether or not there was this agitation by sexless busybodies with nothing better to do than decry everything and everybody ...

I have myself worked at one of these camps when measles and influenza were raging. To children and adults, already debilitated by the results of war, anxiety, bad food and other hardships, any illness would be likely to become serious in the severe winter weather, especially when people are living under canvas; even those in comfortable homes in Johannesburg, Pretoria and other towns suffer.

The Boers in the camps often depend on home remedies, with deplorable results. Inflammation of the lungs and enteric fever are frequently treated by the stomach of a sheep or goat which has been killed at the bedside of a patient being placed hot and bloody over the chest or abdomen; cow-dung poultices are a favourite remedy for many skin diseases; lice are given for jaundice; and crushed bugs for convulsions in children. These are common remedies in everyday use on the farms.

As far as the authorities are concerned, everything is done in the camps that can be done: good food, good clothing and blankets are provided and British soldiers are employed to keep the camps clean, carrying water, serving rations and assisting in every way. It is my firm belief that if the camps had not been established, sickness and mortality would have been far greater on the farms and villages, and even in the towns.

Despite Dr Kay's apologia, some twenty thousand concentration camp inmates had died by the end of the war – a bitter legacy for the ensuing era of reconstruction and reconciliation.

A triumphant General Botha (leading horseman on the left) returning from a successful engagement at Kliprivier, May 1900.

The guerilla war went on while the controversy raged over British methods of counteracting commando tactics. For some British officers the campaign had all the qualities of a pheasant shoot or a tiger hunt, with good 'bags' and big 'drives'. Captain Talbot of the Royal Horse Artillery wrote cheerily in his diary early in 1902:

The capture of Ben Viljoen is a good bag. The general opinion here is that the war ends the day de Wet is collared. Botha wants to chuck but daren't until the Free Staters chuck. An enormous concentration is going on all round de Wet – 25,000 troops at least in about forty columns not to speak of the blockhouses, etc. You can get some idea of the blockhouse lines by taking a map as follows: all railways of course in O.R.C. [Orange River Colony]; a line from Heilbron to Frankfort and Standerton; Kroonstad to Lindley, Bethlehem, Harrismith, Winberg, Senekal and Bethlehem; Bloemfontein, Ladybrand, Basuto border; Orange River and Caledon.

A little later he described another determined British effort to end the war:

> The big drive is over with a total of 850 Boers and all their stock. The bag last week was 1,100, splendid, and two or three more big drives will knock them out. Arthur Scott seems to have done very well in the mountains. Vilonel, the Boer is here now, and takes the field as soon as he gets his men together. He and K. of K. calculate there are 8,000 to 9,000 left. This was before the drive I believe. There is also a rumour that Botha has sent to de Wet and Steyn to say that if they don't chuck it soon, he is going to do so in any case. On the whole things are brightening every day.

But even as Viljoen was in the process of surrendering, Jan Smuts was boldly striking deep into Cape Colony at the head of his commando unit. By the end of February 1902, he was less than 150 miles from Cape Town, and an official report contained some uneasy observations:

> As the forces of the enemy under General Smuts now south of Calvinia appear to be moving in a westerly direction towards Clanwilliam, I am sending a further 100 of the Cape Police to strengthen Major Hennessy. I can spare these for the present as Major Corbett reports the Sutherland district is clear of the enemy ... he states that every farm has furnished its quota to the rebels and that there is hardly a loyal farmer in the district. He further informs me that there are not many supplies left, and the enemy will find it difficult to live for any length of time near there ... the blockhouse line is now completed on the east to beyond Carnarvon ... The general scheme is now to drive the enemy north of the line Clanwilliam, Williston and Victoria West.

Kitchener was anxious to end the war as soon as possible. Not only was the protracted guerilla campaign embarrassing and costly, but he was anxious to take up his next appointment, the plum job of commander-in-chief of the Indian Army. In February 1901 he met Botha at Middleburg in the eastern Transvaal; nothing came of these talks since the British government, partly on the insistence of Alfred Milner at Cape Town, were determined on the principle of unconditional surrender.

In June 1901 F. W. Reitz, State Secretary of the Transvaal government, wrote to President Steyn pointing out that large numbers of Boers were surrendering and wondering if the struggle could be protracted much longer. Steyn, whose Orange Free State had been virtually dragged into the war on the Transvaal's coattails, was resolute, and replied, 'We should be committing the murder of a nation if we were to give in now.'

166   General Schalk Burger. Acting-President of the Transvaal after Kruger's flight.

On 16 December, Lord Rosebery, Liberal-imperialist and a former Prime Minister, said in a speech at Chesterfield that 'some of the greatest peaces in the world's history have begun with an apparently casual meeting of two travellers in a neutral inn, and I think it might well happen that some such fortuitous meeting might take place under the auspices of His Majesty's government and of the exiled Boer government which might lead to very good results'. Perhaps in response to this suggestion the Netherlands' government offered, on 25 January 1902, to act as mediator. The British government did not take up this proposal, but did make it clear that it was prepared to recognize the leaders of those Boers still in the field as the representatives of the fallen Afrikaner republics, rather than those who had already surrendered (like Cronje) or fled abroad (like Kruger).

From 9–11 April 1902 Boer leaders met at Klerksdorp in the south-west Transvaal to discuss whether to negotiate with Kitchener. The Transvaal was represented by Vice-President Schalk Burger, Louis Botha and de la Rey, the Free State by President Steyn, de Wet and Hertzog. Though Steyn and de Wet were for continuing the fight, the Transvaalers were more anxious to negotiate a settlement. At last it was decided to seek a personal meeting with Kitchener. The meeting took place in Pretoria between 12 and 17 April. The Afrikaners wanted a restoration of their independence, but offered a treaty of friendship, a customs and railway union, equal rights for the English and Afrikaans languages, and arbitration for future disputes.

Kitchener was no enthusiast for Milner's call for unconditional surrender, but he was naturally bound by the policy laid down by the British government. The Colonial Secretary, Joseph Chamberlain, would not countenance the restoration of Boer independence and their proposals were thus rejected. Kitchener did, however, manage to establish cordial relations with most of the Afrikaner leaders, especially Botha, whom he considered to be a man who would be 'of valuable assistance to the future Government of the country in an official capacity'. Though he would not agree to an armistice, Kitchener did propose a 'go-slow' to allow the Afrikaner leaders to consult more fully with their men.

In May 1902, sixty Boer delegates (thirty from the Transvaal and thirty from the Free State) met at Vereeniging forty miles south-east of Johannesburg. Jan Smuts also arrived under safe conduct from Cape Province as a legal adviser, having been lobbied by Kitchener on his way to Vereeniging. Kitchener told Smuts that he was prepared to offer surrender with honour, to disarm those

Africans that had been enlisted on the British side, and to ensure that the question of the non-white franchise in the Transvaal and the Free State would be deferred until self-government had been restored to those territories. With the commandos' struggle in the field becoming daily more difficult, and with the growing shortage of horses, arms and supplies, these proposals were attractive ones for the basis of a settlement. On 15 May the Boer leaders began their momentous conference at Vereeniging.

Opposite 'Slim (crafty) Jannie.' Jan Smuts (left) in 1902.

Chapter 10

'No End of a Lesson'

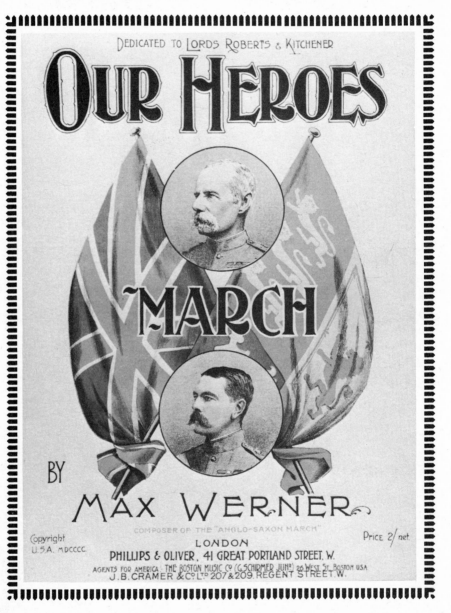

The opening day of the conference at Vereeniging was in great part devoted to a discussion as to whether the Boer delegates had the freedom to make whatever peace they thought the best. Eventually it was decided that delegates should not be bound by the views of those whom they represented.

The conference now got under way. Botha spoke first, and emphasized the plight of his commandos. In less than a year, he claimed, six thousand of his men had either been killed or captured; of the rest, nearly a third had lost their horses and were therefore not effective fighters. He also claimed that the Africans were becoming increasingly hostile and difficult. De Wet and the Free State delegates, backed by Generals Kemp and Beyers from the Transvaal, were more optimistic; they also argued that food could always be taken from the Africans.

On the second day, Acting President Schalk Burger ruled out the possibility of foreign intervention, saying, 'I emphatically state that the war cannot be carried on any longer and I ask if there is any man here who can maintain with a clear conscience that the struggle can be successfully continued?' Botha followed this up by pointing out that large sections of the Transvaal were now incapable of supporting a commando unit. He went on to argue that there was everything to lose by not making a settlement now: 'Terms might now be secured which would save the language, our ancient customs and national ideals. The fatal thing would be to secure no terms at all and yet be forced to surrender.' De la Rey also believed that even the 'bitter-enders' should face facts: 'We have now heard that everything has been sacrificed – cattle, goods, money, wives and children. Our men are going about half naked and some of our women have nothing but skins to wear. Is not this the bitter end?' De Wet would not accept these arguments and chose instead to put his trust in God's steadfast support, but, in this matter at least, the majority of his fellow delegates were now agnostics.

On 17 May the delegates at Vereeniging agreed on peace proposals: the two republics would accept a British Protectorate, and would give up control of foreign policy, the goldfields and Swaziland. On 19 May a five-man delegation, consisting of Botha, de la Rey, Smuts, de Wet and Hertzog, went to Pretoria to negotiate with Kitchener who had now been joined by the implacable Milner. Milner rejected the Boers' proposals outright, and instead called upon them to accept annexation, to become British citizens and to stop all further resistance. He also said that he was not prepared to

Opposite 'Bobs' and 'K' adorn the cover of stirring march-sheet by Max Werner.

draw up a document for the Boers to cut to pieces; instead, they should draw up the terms of an agreement on the basis of his proposals.

De Wet, with characteristic determination, began to object to Milner's dictatorial attitude, but Kitchener saved the situation by saying that the military men should leave such matters to lawyers. A sub-committee was then formed; it consisted of Smuts, Hertzog, Milner and Sir Richard Solomans (Milner's legal adviser). Both Smuts and Hertzog were fully qualified legal men; Smuts indeed had read law at Cambridge University and had been subsequently called to the English Bar. This sub-committee then drew up a legal draft of the peace proposals. During the two days of deliberations that followed, Kitchener privately put it to Smuts that he and his fellow Afrikaners should not see the peace settlement as immutable. After all, Kitchener said, he quite expected to see a Liberal government in Britain within two years, and then the Boers could expect more sympathetic treatment.

On 21 May the final draft was presented to the Afrikaner delegates. Its clauses were as follows: the Boers should lay down their arms and acknowledge King Edward VII as their lawful sovereign; all prisoners, internees, and those at war beyond the annexed republics' frontiers would be allowed to return home, without loss of property or freedom, on making the same acknowledgement; amnesty would be granted to all who surrendered, except those who had committed acts contrary to the usages of war; the Boers could keep their weapons (i.e. rifles), under licence, for personal protection; Dutch (Afrikaans) would be taught in the state schools of the annexed republics where parents so wished, and could be used, where necessary for greater efficiency, in courts of law; military administration would be superseded at the earliest possible date by civil government which would in turn be superseded, as soon as possible, by representative institutions leading to self-government; the question of the 'native franchise' (i.e. votes for non-Europeans in the Transvaal and the Free State) would be decided after the restoration of self-government; no special tax would be levied to cover the cost of the war; district commissions were to be established to assist resettlement, to provide necessities lost in the war, and to honour bank or promissory notes issued by the two republics – for these ends the British government would provide a free gift of £3 million, and loans at low rates of interest after two years and interest-free before then.

In essence these were reasonable terms. Though the two republics were confirmed as crown colonies under direct military rule, the vexed question of non-European enfranchisement was deferred until the white population achieved self-government. In effect, this concession (not a particularly painful one for the British government) meant that the overwhelming Afrikaner majority in the Free State, and even the Afrikaner and British population of the Transvaal would, in all probability, keep the non-European disenfranchised and firmly in his place. Kitchener also gave informal assurances that the Cape rebels would, at the worst, face a temporary loss of voting rights not the firing squad.

On 29 May the delegates assembled to debate the peace terms. President Steyn, old and sick, had already denounced them as a betrayal of the Afrikaner people for £3 million (rather than thirty pieces of silver). The debate was somewhat circumscribed by Milner's announcement that the terms could not be altered and must be either accepted or rejected by midnight on 31 May. President Steyn withdrew, saying that as a sick man he ought to take no further part in the discussion; next morning he appointed de Wet as Acting President.

The debate continued, with the Free Staters the most reluctant to accept the settlement. Smuts made a speech of poignant and intelligent realism:

> If we consider the matter from a military standpoint, if we consider it only as a military matter, then I must admit that we can still go on with the struggle. We are still an unvanquished military force. We have still 18,000 men [the figure was nearer 21,000] in the field, veterans, with whom you can do almost any work. We can thus advance our cause, from a military point of view, still further. But we are not here as an army, but as people; we have not only a military question, but also a national matter to deal with. No one here represents his own commando only. Everyone here represents the Afrikaner people, and not only that portion which is still in the field, but those who are already buried, and those who will live after we are gone. We represent, not only ourselves, but also the thousands who are dead, and have made the last sacrifice for their people, the prisoners of war scattered all over the world, and the men and women who are dying by the thousands in the concentration camps of the enemy; we represent the blood and tears of an entire nation ...
>
> Hitherto we have not pursued the struggle aimlessly. We did not fight merely to be shot at. We began the struggle, and continued it up to this moment because we wished to preserve our independence, and we were prepared to sacrifice everything for it. But we may not sacrifice the Afrikaner people for that independence.

Overleaf Kitchener and de Wet sign the final peace terms in May 1902.

But 31 May came with de Wet and the 'bitter-enders' unshaken in their defiance. Finally, urgent personal appeals by Botha, de la Rey, 173

Smuts and Hertzog won de Wet over; that, and a preamble, composed by Smuts and Hertzog, which was attached to the terms of surrender, and which in effect said that the Boers accepted the terms only because they were forced to do so, and that they looked for prompt improvements in the conditions of their defeated people.

At the last count, fifty-four of the sixty delegates voted for the draft settlement, and the agreement was signed in Pretoria an hour before Milner's ultimatum expired on 31 May. Kitchener shook hands with the Boer leaders, saying 'We are good friends now', but elsewhere some Transvaalers dug a hole for their flag, the Vierkleur, and buried it.

The Peace of Vereeniging ended nearly two years and eight months of war. On 1 June London knew the news and soon the crowds were out 'mafficking' once more. Set beside the holocaust of the Great War the Boer War was a trifling affair in terms of blood and money. Britain lost 21,942 officers and men, and spent £250 million. The Afrikaners lost 3,990 killed in battle and 1,081 more died of wounds and illness; nearly 26,000 died in the concentration camps, – 20,000 of them being under sixteen years of age.

There were, moreover, 31,000 Boer prisoners-of-war, and 116,500 Afrikaners (and over 100,000 non-Europeans) in the concentration camps, while 50,000 Uitlanders who had left Johannesburg now wished to return. The gold mines were idle, with the vast bulk of their black labour force dispersed. The number of cattle had been reduced by half, there were over $3\frac{1}{2}$ million fewer sheep, and 30,000 farms had been burnt down.

The task of reconciliation and reconstruction was a daunting one. Emily Hobhouse left a moving account of conditions in the north of the Orange River Colony (formerly the Orange Free State):

The whole of Lindley is too sad and dejected outwardly to write about ... The Koks are so poor I hardly dared to eat their food; their bed was corrugated iron, the floor would have been pliable by comparison. The ruins of their nice house stand before the door, never alas, to be rebuilt, for they are too old and can never earn the money again. He is seventy-four, but the plucky old man saved the Church registers and stuck to them through thick and thin. He is an educated man. From affluence they are brought in old age to dire poverty. But there was no word of complaint, he spent his time telling me of all the poor around while he said no word of his own condition. I had to learn that from others. It is all lamentable in the town and district ... I fear hope is waning at last, and I dread lest their self-respect should be lost ... About fifteen miles out from town we met a man with a bundle under his arm walking towards Lindley. He had on the green trousers of the Ceylon prisoners of war, and there was purpose on his face. Shortly we came upon his

A. J. Balfour reading the terms of surrender in the House of Commons, 2 June: 'The burgher forces in the field desist from any further resistance to the authority of King Edward VII, whom they recognize as their lawful Sovereign.

little daughter, a child of twelve. She was neatly dressed in a blue print frock and kapje [bonnet], and she was riding a creature which must by courtesy be called a horse. At least it had four legs and a tail and a sort of bone which supported the saddle. She was leading another such animal which had helped to carry her father to town. We called to her to ask the way, and she rode close up to our cart.

She had the motionless face of the veld girl with the deep still eyes, and she sat her horse with grace and self-possession. We had some talk with her.

'How goes it with you?' we said.

'It goes well,' she replied.

'Have you then food?'

'No, we have no food.'

'You mean that you have no meat?'

'No, we have no meat.'

'But you have vegetables or potatoes?'

'No, we have no vegetables.'

'But at least you have bread?'

'No, we have no bread.'

'What! No bread nor meal?'

'No, we have no bread nor meal.'

'Then what do you eat?'

'Just mealies.'

Emily Hobhouse gave the child the only half loaf of bread she had. A little later she and her companion Piet Tante came to a place called Plezier:

A piece of house had been patched up, but there was no smoke or other sign of life. Not a tree or bush or plant or green blade of any sort could be seen near or far. We knocked, seeking permission to outspan. A deadness hung over the place; I felt anxious, I wondered what we should find. Remember, the Boer custom when a cart drives up to the door is for the master or mistress to come out, introduce themselves, and with all heartiness invite you in and make you welcome. After several knocks the door was opened, leave was given us to outspan, but still we were not invited in. I got out of the cart and went to the door. The house was poor but exquisitely neat; there were no chairs, just a table and a box or two to sit upon. Upon the clay walls were fastened the few relics of better days. A good-looking woman and a number of girls, neatly but poorly dressed, were grouped round the room and an equal number of tidy boys in the kitchen at the back. There were eleven children. They sat very silent looking at me, and I introduced myself as coming from well-known men in their town. Mr Theron wanted to take our luncheon in the house, but some instinct told me there was great trouble there and I could not eat with all those eyes upon me. So I only asked permission to boil my kettle on their table out of the wind, and then when we had lunched I said I would come and hear their story. I hated myself afterwards to think I had made my tea at their table. When I made them understand who I was, the women told me all – the same sad tale, of

course, as everywhere, but they had nothing left, nothing to eat but mealies, and so few of them that they must eke them out by one meal a day only. There was nowhere to turn for money or for help; the husband had tramped away some thirty miles to seek work on a railway; at best he would get 4s. 6d. a day, and on that no family here can live; it would not much more than feed him …

One of the girls took me into the bedroom and in a whisper told me they had nothing to eat. The woman kept her secret longer. It is so awful to people of this good class to say they are in want, or even seem to beg …

This man was a very fine young Boer with well cut features. His young wife was with him. Mr Theron introduced me to them; they belong to a good family, as indeed was apparent by their dress and bearing. The woman put her arm through mine and whispered she wanted to speak to me. She drew me out of earshot of the men on the stoep [verandah].

Victory parade of Colonial Mounted Infantry; Pall Mall East, 31 May 1902.

179

Then her courage failed her and she could not speak. Her face was very white with blue shadows round the lips and eyes. I said, 'Are you hungry?' I am getting experienced now and begin to understand. She said for months she had eaten nothing but mealies, not meal, nor meat, nor coffee, nor anything else. They had borrowed the cart and come to the store to fetch the last half bag they could buy. She put her hand on my arm again and said, 'I have nothing, we have nothing, don't you understand?' And then at last I did understand, her baby was coming, the first baby, and she had not even a shawl to wrap it in. I understood her Dutch perfectly, but she was too shy to speak openly. She said she had a frightful craving for a bit of fresh meat, but none was to be got in the shop. A baby's shawl and a bit of flannelette made heaven open for her again, and I gave her a tin of Australian mutton and a few groceries. She has a good face. Six of her brothers and sisters had died in Kroonstad Camp.

Alfred Milner dominated the first years of reconstruction, until his return to the United Kingdom in 1905. Thwarted in his design forcibly to bring about a federation in South Africa, he did his best to ensure that British supremacy, so painfully asserted during the war, should be maintained in the foreseeable future. A customs union, including Rhodesia, was established in 1903, and Milner tried hard to promote the English language, and to saturate the local civil services with British citizens. But the floods of anticipated British emigrants did not arrive. 'Milnerization', in fact, was a failure. Britain had won the war, but almost at once started to lose the peace.

In December 1905 Balfour's Unionist government resigned. Campbell-Bannerman became Prime Minister; in the election of January 1906 the Liberals annihilated their opponents. Kitchener's prophecy of 1902 was now fulfilled, for in February 1906 the government announced in the speech from the throne that self-government would be given forthwith to the Transvaal and the Orange River Colony. In February 1907 elections for the Transvaal's new assembly gave an overall majority of five seats to Het Volk, the Afrikaner party led by Louis Botha and Jan Smuts. In March, Botha was installed as the first Prime Minister of the self-governing colony of the Transvaal. The Uitlanders, as unreliable after the war as before it, had split their vote between the Progressive and Labour parties, and had thus helped Het Volk to its victory. Soon afterwards the Afrikaner Oranjia Unie party predictably swept the board in elections in the Orange River Colony.

Within two years a Bill for the Union of South Africa was before the British Parliament, and on 1 January 1910 Botha became the first Prime Minister of the new Union, which took its place as a

A flurry of patriotic handkerchieves. Blow your nose for Britain!

self-governing dominion within the British Empire. In 1919 he was succeeded by another Boer general Jan Smuts, who was in turn replaced by a third ex-commando leader, J. B. Hertzog, in 1924. It hardly seemed, therefore, that in political terms the Afrikaner commando leaders had done badly out of their protracted resistance.

It is also clear that the Afrikaners had fought a good war. Certainly their casualties were lower. It had perhaps been strategically crippling for them to concentrate so heavily on the sieges of Ladysmith, Mafeking and Kimberley when bolder thrusts into the Cape and Natal might have shattered British morale. In any case, Roberts and Kitchener ignored the railway network obsession of the early months of the war, and turned the Boer position with sweeping and adventurous outflanking movements. But the Afrikaners, with their limited manpower, were probably right to stick close to easily defended hill positions rather than risk a stand-up fight on the veld where their opponents would stand a better chance of effectively concentrating and using the different arms of their forces. The guerilla war after Paardeberg, however, shows how outstandingly successful small forces of commandos were even when deployed over huge distances.

Man for man, the short-service British recruits were far less versatile and intuitive than their civilian opponents, and their shooting rarely approached the deadly accuracy of the Boers'. The British troops were, however, generally courageous and steadfast in adversity, whereas the free and easy democratic character of the commando units sometimes led to easy demoralization and dispersal when things began to go badly wrong. It is also odd that, for all their tactical success, commanders like Botha had sometimes to cajole and browbeat their men into action whereas, for all his stumblings and defeats, Buller retained the warm regard of his rank and file.

In the last resort, the British emerged from the war with one positive advantage. The tactical fiascos and deficiencies in supply and training prompted an avalanche of military reform, and many of the recommendations of a variety of commissions of enquiry were acted upon. Although these reforms did not transform the officer class into military geniuses overnight, or create subtle, hardened campaigners out of the enlisted men, they at least helped to make the British army a better organized fighting machine when the Great War broke out in August 1914.

The Boer War did one other service to Britain and her Empire. It pricked the inflated bubble of *fin de siècle* jingoism and recalled the British nation to more sober imperial judgements and perspectives.

Kipling put it cogently when he wrote in 'The Lesson, 1899–1902':

Let us admit it fairly as a business people should,
We have had no end of a lesson: it will do us no end of good.

Not on a single issue, or in one direction or twain,
But conclusively, comprehensively, and several times and again,
Were all our most holy illusions knocked higher than Gilderoy's kite.
We have had a jolly good lesson, and it serves us jolly well right!

We have spent two hundred million pounds to prove the fact once more,
That horses are quicker than men afoot, since two and two make four;
And horses have four legs, and men have two legs, and two into four
    goes twice.
And nothing over except our lesson – and very cheap at the price.

It was our fault, and our very great fault – and now we must turn it to
    use.
We have forty million reasons for failure, but not a single excuse.
So the more we work and the less we talk the better results we shall get.
We have had an Imperial lesson. It may make us an Empire yet!

The international animosity felt for Britain during the war proved to be merely a passing, though virulent, spasm. 'Splendid isolation' was in fact being ditched as the Boers prepared to surrender at Vereeniging. In 1902 the Anglo-Japanese Alliance was signed; in 1904 (the year Kruger died in Switzerland) the Anglo-French Entente took place, followed in 1907 by a British entente with Russia. In any case, there were soon other international conflicts to attract attention: the Russo-Japanese War of 1904–5, for example, and the 1905 Moroccan crisis.

What of the British commanders who had between them displayed such a mixture of incompetence and resolution in South Africa? Buller lapsed into a well deserved obscurity; Lord Roberts barely survived the outbreak of the Great War; Lord Kitchener, a ponderous Secretary of State for War, was drowned in a Baltic shipwreck in 1916; Sir John French, so dashing and decisive on the veld, fumbled as Commander of the British Expeditionary Force in 1914 and was eventually replaced by another Boer War officer, Sir Douglas Haig; Baden-Powell made his name synonomous, not with the defence of Mafeking, but with the world scouting movement; Sir George White became a field-marshal and received the Order of Merit in 1905 despite Prime Minister Arthur Balfour's judgement that 'though the OM would add to his reputation, I do not think that he would add to the reputation of the OM.'

The war left the British people with a host of ephemera. Biscuit tins with Buller's portly frame stamped upon them, a new word for

LOCAL LIEUTENANT GENERAL IAN HAMILTON
COMMANDING MOUNTED INFANTRY DIVISION.

MAJOR GENERAL R.S.S. BADEN POWELL
DEFENDER OF MAFEKING.

MAJOR GENERAL J.D.P. FRENCH
COMMANDING CAVALRY DIVISION.

MAJOR GENERAL SIR H.M. LESLIE RUNDLE
COMMANDING 8TH DIVISION.

MAJOR GENERAL LORD KITCHENER OF KHARTOUM
CHIEF OF THE STAFF.

MAJOR GENERAL SIR ARCHIBALD HUNTER
COMMANDING 10TH DIVISION.

LIEUTENANT GENERAL LORD METHUEN
COMMANDING FIRST DIVISION.

A. HUGH FISHER. 1900.

184   British Commanders in the Boer War.

the language, a coven of semi-diabolic foes – Kruger, Cronje and the rest, and here and there a Spion Kop, a Buller Road or a Kitchener Avenue. In the music halls they had earlier bade farewell to Dolly Gray, but a little later comics were welcoming a newly christened citizen:

> The baby's name is Kitchener Carrington
> Methuen Kekewich White
> Cronje Plumer Powell Majuba
> Gatacre Warren Colenso Kruger
> Capetown Mafeking French
> Kimberley Ladysmith Bobs
> Union Jack Fighting Mac
> Lyddite Pretoria BLOBBS.

The Boer War virtually completed Britain's annexations in Africa. From the Cape to Cairo, from Kenya to Gambia, the map was daubed with red. Yet no warrior tribe in the whole continent had given one fraction of the resistance offered by the Afrikaners of the Transvaal and the Orange Free State. Ironically, within sixty years of the end of the Boer War, Britain's African empire had disintegrated, and unified South Africa, now a republic, had withdrawn from the Commonwealth of Nations. At this last, at least, the ghosts of Kruger and de Wet must have taken some quiet satisfaction.

Glossary

African: black-skinned native of Southern Africa; sometimes called 'Bantu'.

Afrikaans: the language spoken by the Afrikaners, which evolved from Dutch.

Afrikaner: one descended from settlers of Dutch, Huguenot, Flemish or German stock, and living in South Africa.

Boer: British term used to describe the Afrikaners; true meaning 'farmer'; a term of abuse.

Dorp: small town or village.

Drift: ford across a river.

Kaffir: strictly a particular tribe, but used as a term of abuse for all Africans in South Africa.

Kopje: small hill, hill

Kraal: African settlement or stock enclosure.

Laager: encampment.

Nek: mountain pass, or break in hills.

Outspan: to unyoke oxen from wagon.

South Africa: not a unified state until 1910; general term used to describe southern Africa prior to that.

South African Republic: the Transvaal's official title.

Spruit: stream, small river.

Stoep: verandah.

Veld: the open countryside.

Zarp: the South African Republic's police force.

NB The English spelling of 'Spion' Kop has been used throughout.

Select
Bibliography

Amery, L. S. (ed.), *The Times History of the War in South Africa*, 7 vols (London, 1900–9).

Churchill, W. S., *My Early Life* (London, 1930).

Comaroff, John L. (ed.), *The Boer War Diary of Sol T. Plaatje* (London, 1973).

Conan Doyle, Arthur, *The Great Boer War* (London, 1902).

De Wet, C., *Three Years' War* (London, 1903).

Fisher, J., *Paul Kruger* (London, 1974).

Fisher, J., *The Afrikaners* (London, 1969).

Gardner, Brian, *Mafeking: A Victorian Legend* (London, 1966).

Gardner, Brian, *The Lion's Cage: Cecil Rhodes and the Siege of Kimberley* (London, 1969).

Griffiths, K., *Thank God We Kept the Flag Flying* (London, 1974).

Hancock, Keith, *Smuts*, vol 1 (Cambridge, 1962).

Holt, E., *The Boer War* (London, 1962).

Judd, Denis, *Balfour and the British Empire* (London, 1968).

Judd, Denis, *Someone Has Blundered* (London, 1973).

Kruger, Rayne, *Goodbye Dolly Gray* (London, 1959).

Le May, G. H. L., *British Supremacy in South Africa* (London, 1965).

Magnus, Philip, *Kitchener: Portrait of an Imperialist* (London, 1958).

Marais, J. S., *The Fall of Kruger's Republic* (Oxford, 1961).

May, H. J., *Music of the Guns* (London, 1970).

Meintjes, J., *General Louis Botha* (London, 1970).

Meintjes, J., *Stormberg* (Cape Town, 1969).

Pemberton, W. B., *Battles of the Boer War* (London, 1964).

Ransford, Oliver, *The Battle of Spion Kop* (London, 1969).

Reitz, D., *Commando* (London, 1903).

Roberts, Brian, *Churchills in Africa* (London, 1970).

Selby, John, *The Boer War* (London, 1969).

Symons, Julian, *Buller's Campaign* (London, 1963).

Wilson, H. W., *With the Flag to Pretoria*, 2 vols (London, 1901).

Index